George A. Henty

A chapter of adventures

Through the bombardment of Alexandria

George A. Henty

A chapter of adventures
Through the bombardment of Alexandria

ISBN/EAN: 9783744785723

Printed in Europe, USA, Canada, Australia, Japan

Cover: Foto ©ninafisch / pixelio.de

More available books at **www.hansebooks.com**

A CHAPTER OF ADVENTURES;

OR, THROUGH THE BOMBARDMENT OF ALEXANDRIA.

A CHAPTER OF ADVENTURES

OR,

THROUGH THE BOMBARDMENT OF ALEXANDRIA

BY

G. A. HENTY,

Author of "By Pike and Dyke;" "The Lion of St. Mark;" "The Cat of Bubastes;"
"Bonnie Prince Charlie;" "By England's Aid;" &c.

WITH SIX FULL-PAGE ILLUSTRATIONS BY
W. H. OVEREND.

GLASGOW:
BLACKIE & SON, Limited.
TORONTO:
WILLIAM BRIGGS, 29-33 Richmond St. West.
THE COPP, CLARK COMPANY, Limited, 9 Front St. West.

Entered according to Act of the Parliament of Canada, in the year one thousand eight hundred and ninety-nine, by BLACKIE & SON, Limited, at the Department of Agriculture.

CONTENTS.

Chap		Page
I.	A Fishing Village,	9
II.	Caught by the Tide,	24
III.	A Run from Harwich,	40
IV.	The Wreck,	54
V.	The Rescue,	67
VI.	Altered Prospects,	82
VII.	On Board the "Wild Wave,"	97
VIII.	Alexandria,	110
IX.	The Riot in Alexandria,	124
X.	Prisoners,	139
XI.	The Bombardment,	153
XII.	Free,	168
XIII.	Among Friends,	183
XIV.	A Set of Rascals,	198
XV.	A Threatening Sky,	212
XVI.	Old Joe's Yarn,	224
XVII.	In Dangerous Seas,	246
XVIII.	A Cyclone,	261
XIX.	Cast Ashore,	275

ILLUSTRATIONS

	Page
WAITING FOR HELP, ... *Frontispiece.*	37
JACK REACHES THE SPAR, ...	68
THE FIGHT WITH THE EGYPTIAN RIOTERS, ...	132
THE THREE LADS WITNESS THE BOMBARDMENT, ...	164
"SURRENDER," JIM SHOUTED, "OR WE FIRE!"	207
CAUGHT IN THE CYCLONE, ...	274

A CHAPTER OF ADVENTURES.

CHAPTER I.

A FISHING VILLAGE.

OF the tens of thousands of excursionists who every summer travel down by rail to Southend, there are few indeed who ever stop at Leigh, or who, once at Southend, take the trouble to walk three miles along the shore to the fishing village. It may be doubted, indeed, whether along the whole stretch of coast-line from Plymouth to Yarmouth there is a village that has been so completely overlooked by the world. Other places, without a tithe of its beauty of position, or the attraction afforded by its unrivalled view over the Thames, from Gravesend to Warden Point, ever alive with ships passing up and down, have grown from fishing hamlets to fashionable watering-places; while Leigh remains, or at any rate remained at the time this story opens, ten years ago, as unchanged and unaltered as if, instead of being but an hour's run from London, it lay far north in Scotland.

Its hill rises steeply behind it; there is room only for the street between the railway and the wharves, and for a single row of houses between the line and the foot of the hill. To get into Leigh from the country round it is necessary to descend by a steep road that winds down from the church at the top of the hill; to get out again you must go by the same way. The population is composed solely of fishermen, their families, and the shopkeepers who supply their necessities. The men who stand in groups in the street and on the wharf are all clad in blue guernseys or duck smocks and trousers of pilot cloth or canvas. Broad-built sturdy men are they, for in point of physique there are few fishermen round the coast who can compare with those of Leigh.

A stranger in the place would think that the male population had nothing to do but to stand in the street and talk, but night is for the most part their time for work; although many of the bawleys go out on the day-tide also, for at Leigh the tide is all-important. For five hours in the day it washes the foot of the wharves, for seven a wide expanse of mud stretches away to Canvey Island in front, and Southend Pier to the east.

At the wells—for Leigh still depends for water on its wells—are, during the hours at which water is permitted to be drawn, lines of twenty women and girls with pails, each patiently waiting her turn. There are not many boys about, for boys require more sleep than men, and a considerable portion of their time on shore is spent in bed.

It is ten o'clock in the day; the bawleys have returned from the fishing grounds, and scores of them have anchored in the Ray—a deep stretch of water lying between the spit of sand that extends from the end of Canvey Island close up to Southend Pier, and the mud-flats of Leigh. The flats are still uncovered, but the tide is rising fast in the winding channel leading up to the village. In a few minutes there will be water enough for the boats, and already these can be seen leaving the bawleys and making for the mouth of the channel. The wind is fair, and each boat hoists its sail, white or yellow or brown, and with the crew sitting up to windward comes flying along the shallow channel, making, as they always do, a race of it home.

The boats are large and roomy, and are, as they need to be, good sea-boats; for they have at times to live in rough water that would swamp lighter craft like cockle-shells. Each boat carries two men and a boy, that being the regular crew of a bawley; although, perhaps, for rough winter work, they may sometimes take an extra hand. In the bow of the first boat that comes tearing along up to the wharf sits a good-looking lad, about fourteen years old. His face is bronzed with the sun and wind, his clothes are as rough and patched as those of the other fisher lads; but although as strong and sinewy as any of his companions of the same age, he is somewhat slighter in his build, more active in his movements, and has a more springy and elastic walk in spite of the heavy boots that he wears.

He helps the others to land several baskets of shrimps, and carry them to the railway-station hard by. They are already boiled, for the bawleys carry coppers, into which the shrimps are baled straight from the nets, so that they are in readiness to send off to town as soon as they are landed. When the baskets are all piled on the platform he crosses the line, follows it along for some fifty yards, and then enters a neat cottage facing it.

"Back again all safe, Jack?"

"All right, mother! It's been a fine night, with just enough wind, and not too much. I ought to have been in half an hour ago, but tide is late this morning."

"Lily brought word, just as she was starting for school, that the boats were coming up the creek, so your breakfast is all ready."

"And so am I, mother; though I had a piece of bread and cheese when we dropped anchor. I will just wash my hands, and be ready in a jiffey."

Mrs. Robson was a native of Leigh. Her father had been a fisherman, who had owned his own bawley; indeed, most of the boats at Leigh are the property of one of the men who work them.

Bessy Tripper—not that her real name was Tripper, but Snow; but her father for some unknown reason got the nickname of Tripper, and his sons and daughters were also called by it, and would hardly have answered if addressed as Snow—was one of the prettiest girls in Leigh; so thought William Robson, a young artist, who came down to Leigh to spend the summer there, sketching the picturesque boats as they came in and out, or lay, with their heads pointing all round the compass, on the soft mud.

He had taken lodgings at Tripper's house, and when not at work with his brush spent much of his time on board the *Enterprise*. Bessy Tripper was a conspicuous figure in the foreground of many of his sketches, and occupied as prominent a place in his thoughts. She was as sweet-tempered as she was pretty, and at last Will Robson made up his mind to marry her if she would take him. He was himself an orphan, and had no friends who had any right to object to his marrying according to his fancy, and he could therefore do as he pleased without question or comment. Bessy Tripper was quite ready to take him when he asked her, and they were married at the church at the top of the hill, and went to live at a little cottage near Dulwich.

William Robson was no genius; he had the knack of painting pretty marine sketches in watercolours. These sold readily, but at low prices; and although he was always talking of doing a great picture in oils that was to make his fortune, the picture never was painted. He was always too busy at what he called pot-boilers, which had to be sold to dealers for a trifle, in order to enable him to meet the butcher and baker's bills. He never repented his marriage; Bessy was an admirable housewife, and made a shilling go as far as many women would a half-crown. In the summer they generally went down for a couple of months to Leigh, for her to see her friends, for him to gather a fresh stock of new subjects.

He died suddenly from the effects of a chill, and when his affairs were wound up Bessy found herself mistress of the five hundred pounds for which he had insured his life, and the furniture of the cottage. It was natural that she should return to Leigh. She had no friends elsewhere; and she knew that money went much further there than in most other places. Two hundred pounds were spent in purchasing the cottage in which she now lived, and another two hundred in buying a bawley. At Leigh, as at most other fishing places, the men work on shares—the boat takes a share, and each of the men a share—the owner of a boat supplying nets as well as the boat itself. The bawley, therefore, brought Mrs. Robson in a sum equal to that earned by a fisherman, with deductions, however, for damages to nets and spars.

In good seasons the receipts sufficed to keep her and her boy and girl comfortably; in bad seasons they had to live very closely, and she was obliged in specially bad times to dip a little into her reserve of a hundred pounds. Upon the other hand, there was occasionally a windfall when the smack rendered assistance to a vessel on the sands, or helped to get up anchors or discharge cargoes.

At the time of her husband's death Jack was ten years old and Lily eight. For two years the former attended the school on the hill, and then went as a boy on board a bawley belonging to one of his uncles.

The lad's own predilections were entirely for the sea, his happiest times had been spent at Leigh, and his father's work had kept the longing alive at other times. He would have preferred going to sea in one of the ships of which there was always such a line passing up and down the river, but he was too young for that when he first began his work on board the bawley; and as the time went on, and he became accustomed to the life of a fisherman, his longings for a wider experience gradually faded away, for it is seldom indeed that a Leigh boy goes to sea—the Leigh men being as a race devoted to their homes, and regarding with grave disapproval any who strike out from the regular groove.

"We did well this morning, mother," Jack said

as he came downstairs in a clean guernsey and pilot trousers. "We had a fine haul off the lower Blyth, and not a bad one higher up. I fancy most of the boats did well. The *Hope* was close to us, and I expect she must have done as well as we did."

"That's good news, Jack. The catches have not been heavy lately, but now they have once begun I hope that we shall have a better time of it."

The breakfast was fish, for fish is the chief article of diet at Leigh.

"Are you going to bed, Jack?"

"No, mother; I did not start until half-past one, and so I got a good six hours before I turned out. I am going to help Uncle Ben put a fresh coat of pitch on our boat. He is going to bring her in as soon as there is water enough. Tom stopped on board with him, but they let me come ashore in Atkins' boat; and of course I lent them a hand to get their fish up. We shall land our lot when the bawley comes up."

"Then you won't go out again to-night, Jack?"

"Oh, yes, we shall, mother. We shall go out with the tide as usual. We shall only do up to the water-line, and the pitch will be plenty dry enough by night. We are going to fish over by Warden Point, I think."

"I am glad to hear it," his mother said. "I always feel more comfortable when you are on that ground, as you are out of the track of steamers there."

"Uncle is talking of going down to Harwich next week."

Mrs. Robson's face fell. She had expected the news, for every year a considerable number of the Leigh bawleys go down to Harwich and fish off that port for two or three months. The absence of Jack was always a great trial to her. When he was with her she felt that he was safe, for it is an almost unheard-of thing for a bawley to meet with an accident when fishing in the mouth of the Thames; but off Harwich the seas are heavy, and although even there accidents are rare—for the boats are safe and staunch and the fishermen handle them splendidly—still the risk is greater than when working at home.

The Leigh men themselves attribute their freedom from accident in no slight degree to the fact that their boats never go out on Sunday. They are God-fearing men these fishermen, and however bad the times, and however hard the pinch, it is seldom indeed that a bawley puts out from Leigh on Sunday, save to the assistance of a vessel in distress.

The excursionists who go down in summer weather to Margate and Ramsgate scarcely think that ships could be cast away and broken up upon the hidden sands beneath the sparkling waters. They know not that scarce one of these sands but at low water is dotted with low, black timbers, and that there are few more dangerous pieces of navigation in the world than the passage up the mouth of the Thames on a wild night when a fierce gale is blowing and the snow and sleet driving before it, obscuring the guiding lights that mark the channels between the sands.

The *Bessy*—for so Ben Tripper had named his bawley, after his favourite sister—was lying on the mud just above Leigh. A fishy smell pervaded the air, for close by were the boiling-sheds, with their vast heaps of white cockle-shells. These were dug by the cocklers either from the sand at the end of the Canvey Island or on the Maplin Sands somewhere off Shoebury.

The large boats often return deeply laden with them. On reaching Leigh the cockles are thrown out in great heaps by the side of the creek, where they are covered at each tide. Here they are left to clean themselves, and to get rid of the sand they have taken in when burrowing. Two or three days later they are carried up to the boiling-houses and thrown into great coppers of boiling water. They open at once, and the fish drop from the shells. The contents of the coppers are passed through large meshed sieves, to allow the fish to pass through and retain the shells, which go to add to the heaps outside. These heaps would in time rival in size the cinder tips of the Midlands were it not that there is a use for the shells. They make splendid lime, and are sometimes taken away in barge-loads and carried to town, where they are used instead of gravel in the parks, making, when crushed, the whitest and tidiest of paths.

Before starting Jack had put on a canvas jumper, leggings and high boots, and was soon at work with his uncle, ankle-deep in the mud. The bawleys are boats almost peculiar to Leigh, although a few hail from Gravesend and the Medway. They are from thirty to forty-five feet long, and are divided into three classes of from six to fifteen tons burden. They are very broad in comparison to their length, some of them having a beam of fifteen feet, and they carry their width almost to the stern, which is square. This gives the boats a dumpy appearance, as they look as if they had been cut short. They are half-decked, with a roomy fo'castle and a well, where the fish are kept alive. They carry one mast.

The peculiarity of their rig is that they have no boom to their mainsail, which in shape somewhat resembles a barge-sail, and, like it, can in a moment be brailed completely up. They carry a lofty topmast and large topsails, and these they seldom lower, even when obliged to have two reefs in the mainsail. They are capital sea-boats, fast, and very handy; and it requires a good yacht to beat a bawley with a brisk wind blowing. The men are keen sailors, and when the trawls are taken up and their heads turned homewards it is always a race to be first back.

Ten years ago all the bawleys were clinker-built—that is, with the streaks overlapping each other, as in boats; but the new bawleys are now all carvel-built, the planks being placed edge to edge, so as to give a smooth surface, as in yachts and large vessels. They now for the most part carry spinnakers, boomed out when running before the wind, and balloon foresails, thereby greatly adding to their speed in light winds. One peculiarity of the bawleys is that, when at anchor, the mainsail, instead of being stowed with its spars parallel to the deck, is made up on its gaff, which is then hoisted with the throat seven or eight feet up the mast, while the peak rests on the stern.

This is done to give more room on deck, and enable the men to get more easily in and out of the fo'castle. It has, however, a curious appearance, and a fleet of bawleys at anchor resembles nothing so much as a flock of broken-backed ducks.

Ben Tripper and his mate, Tom Hoskins, finished tarring the boat under her water-line soon after four o'clock in the afternoon, Jack's share of the work consisting in keeping the fire blazing under the pitch kettle.

"What time shall we go out, uncle?"

"Not going out at all, Jack. We will finish tarring her the first thing in the morning, and there are two or three odd jobs want doing."

"Will you want me, uncle? because, if not, I shall go out early with Bill Corbett cockling. His father has hurt his leg, and is laid up, so he asked me to lend him a hand. I told him I didn't know whether you were going out again to-night or whether you could spare me in the morning, but that if you didn't want me I would go with him."

"You can go, Jack; besides, you will be in early anyhow. We will do the tarring without you."

CHAPTER II.

CAUGHT BY THE TIDE.

JACK ran home.

"I thought you would have been in by two o'clock, Jack," his mother said reproachfully, "so as to see Lily before she went off to school again."

"So I should have done, mother, but I had to stick at the work until we had finished up to the water-line. Uncle Ben thought it was not worth while knocking off."

Jack's meal of bread and bacon was soon finished, then he waited a little until Lily had returned from school.

"Come on, Lil," he said; "I have been waiting to take you out with me."

"Be in by six," Mrs. Robson said.

"All right, mother! We are only just going down to the shore."

Near the little coast-guard station they came upon Bill Corbett.

"Can you come to-morrow, Jack?"

"Yes; uncle has agreed to do without me. What time are you going to start?"

"We will go out as late as we can, Jack. We can get down the creek till three anyhow, so at three o'clock you be ready down here."

"Joe is going, I suppose?"

"Oh, yes, he does to carry the cockles to the boat while we scrape them out. That is a nice bawley, that new one there; she only came in this tide. That is the boat Tom Parker has had built at Brightlingsea. He expects she is going to beat the fleet. She will want to be a rare good one if she does, and I don't think Tom is the man to get the most out of her anyhow."

"I don't reckon he is," Jack agreed. "He would never have bought that boat out of his own earnings, that is certain. It is lucky for him his uncle in town died and left him four hundred pounds. He is one of the lazy ones, he is. Half the times he never goes out at all. It is either too rough, or there ain't wind enough, or he don't think it is a likely day for fish. His mother will do a sight better now that he has got a boat of his own, and she will get someone else to work hers. I should not like to work on shares with him though he has got a new boat and gear."

"Well, I must be going," Bill said. "Shall I knock at your door as I pass in the morning?"

"You will find me there as the clock strikes three, Bill; but if I ain't, you knock."

Bill Corbett, who was a lad some two years older than Jack, strolled away. Jack and Lily sat down on the sloping stage from which the coast-guardsmen launched their boats, and began to chat to the man standing with a telescope under his arm at the door of the boat-shed. Jack was very fond of talking to the coast-guardsmen. They had not, like the fishermen, spent all their lives between Gravesend and Harwich, but had sailed with big ships and been to foreign parts. One of them had been in the China War, another had fought in India with Peel's Naval Brigade, had helped batter down the palace fortresses of Lucknow, and when in the humour they had plenty of tales of stirring incident to relate.

Jack was a favourite with the coast-guardsmen, for he possessed the virtue rare in boys of being able to sit still; and as his favourite place was the slip in front of the boat-house, and he would sit there cutting out toy boats by the hour, he generally came in for a good deal of talk with the men who happened to be on duty. This afternoon, however, the men were busy burnishing up their arms and getting everything into apple-pie order, as the inspecting officer was to come on his rounds the next morning; so Jack after a time strolled along the path between the railway and the track, Lily prattling by his side and stopping to gather wild convolvulus and grasses. The sea was out now, and the mud stretched away, glistening red and brown in the sunlight. Beyond in the Ray lay a long line of bawleys, while a score or more nearer at hand lay heeled over on the mud as they had been left by the receding tide.

To a stranger the black hulks would have looked exactly like each other; but the Leigh men could tell every boat afloat or ashore, even without looking at the number painted on her bulwarks, just as a shepherd can pick out one sheep from a flock.

"It is time to go back, Lily," Jack said at last. "Mother said we were to be in at six, and it cannot be far off that now. There is the Yarmouth steamer going up. It is about her time."

"How do you know it is the Yarmouth steamer, Jack?"

"Oh, I don't know. I know her by her look. I know pretty near all of them—the Yarmouth, the Scotch, and the Dutch boats."

"They all look to me alike."

"Ah! that is because they are a long way off, Lily. There is a lot of difference between them when you are close. We know them all, and which whistles if we are in the way, and which will give way for us, and which will come right on without minding whether they run us down or not. The colliers are the worst for that, they just go straight on, and expect you to get out of the way, and don't mind a rap about the rule of the road or anything else. I should like to see half a dozen of those captains hanged."

"I do not think it is right to say that, Jack."

"Well, I should like to see them get five dozen lashes anyhow," Jack said, "well laid on by some of our fishermen. They would give it 'em heartily, and it would do them a world of good, and save many a life afterwards. It is too bad the way those fellows go on; they don't care a bit about running down a small craft in the dark. In the first place, they know very well that they are not likely to be recognized, and so steam straight on, and leave men to drown; and in the next, if they are recognized, they are ready to swear that black is white all round, and will take their oaths you hadn't got your side-lights burning, or that you changed your course, and that they did all in their power to prevent a collision. I wish some of the people of the Board of Trade would come down the river sometimes in sailing-boats and see the way these coasters set the law at defiance, and fine them smartly. What is the use of making rules if they are never observed? Well, here we are home, and the church is just striking six, so we have hit off the time nicely."

By eight o'clock Jack was in bed, and having acquired the fisherman's habit of waking at any hour he chose, he was at the door when Bill Corbett and his brother Joe came along. The day was already breaking faintly in the east, for the month was May.

"Going to be fine, Bill?" Jack asked.

"Dunno. Wind is blowing strong from the north, though we don't feel it here."

The water was off the flats and had sunk some distance in the creek.

"It is lower than I expected," Bill said. "Come on; come on."

"Where is she, Bill?"

"Close to the foot of the steps."

The boat had already taken ground; but Bill, getting into the water with his high boots, shoved her off. The mast was stepped and sail hoisted, and she was soon running fast down the creek.

"The boats were off an hour ago, I suppose?" Jack remarked.

"Ay, more than that. Some of them turned out at half-past one. But those whose boats were down the channel didn't go for half an hour later. Father told me. I saw him before I started. He couldn't sleep with the pain in his leg."

Twenty minutes' sailing took them down to the mouth of the creek and into the wider channel. They now turned the boat's head directly off shore, and jibed the sail, and bore off for the sands stretching away from the end of Canvey Island.

"No other boats here this morning?" Jack asked as the boat ran ashore.

"No; three or four of them went down to Shoebury last night. They say there is more cockles down there than there is here now. But father said we had best come here. I suppose he thought that Joe, you, and me, made but a poor cocklers' crew. Of course, with the wind blowing off shore, it is all right anyhow; but men never think us boys can do anything. Why, I would not mind a bit starting, us three, for Harwich. I reckon these boats are just as safe as the bawleys?"

"I think so too; but they want more handling. However, I expect we could manage it."

They had now got out their implements, consisting of a shovel, a large rake, and a couple of baskets, on shore, and fastening the boat with a grapnel, went to the place where experience had taught them it was best to dig, and were soon at work. The cockles were for the most part buried some five or six inches in the sand, and were found in great numbers; the two elder boys digging and raking while Joe picked them up, and threw them into the baskets. As these were filled Bill carried them down on his shoulder to the boat, put the baskets into the water, gave them a heave or two to wash some of the sand off the cockles, and then emptied them into the boat.

It was a broad-beamed craft, of over twenty feet long, and would carry more than a ton of cockles if filled up.

The sun had long been up, the clouds were flying fast across the sky, and the wind was working round to the east, knocking up a short choppy sea as it met the ebb, and covering the river with white horses.

The boys worked away sturdily, ceasing occasionally from their labours to go down and shove the boat further off as the tide fell. At six it was dead low. They had each brought with them a bag with some bread and cheese, and a tin of cold tea, and now sat down on the gunwale of the boat for breakfast. Having finished that meal, they continued their work till nine o'clock, by which time they had got several bushels on board.

"Look there!" Joe exclaimed suddenly; "there is a big steamer has run on to the Middle Ground."

The boys had just thrown down their spade and rake, and had agreed to knock off, and they now ran across to the outside of the strip of sand, which had by this time narrowed very considerably.

"She will get off easy enough as the tide rises," Joe said; "but they won't be able to back her off now."

"No; she does not move in the least," Jack agreed. "Her screw is working hard astern now. Look how high her head is. She has run a long way up with wind and tide and steam. She must have gone on it hard."

"She had best get a couple of anchors out astern," Bill said, "before she gets broadside on."

This was evidently also the view of the captain, as two boats were lowered and anchors got into them. But it is no easy matter to row a boat with a heavy weight in it against wind and tide; and before they had got fairly away from the vessel she had already swung round a considerable distance, and was heeling over a good deal from the force of the wind and tide. It was nearly half an hour before the boats were far enough off to get the anchors over with any effect.

"They won't dare to haul on them now," Joe said. "They would only come home. Those anchors ain't heavy enough to work her stern round. I expect when a tug comes along they will get them to help, else she will keep on driving higher and higher."

"Hallo!" The exclamation came from Jack, who now happened to look round towards the boat. They had accidentally taken their stand on the highest point of the sand-bank, and in watching the steamer had forgotten all about the tide, which, under the influence of a north-east wind, had risen with great rapidity. The patch of dry sand was scarcely fifteen yards wide, and would be entirely covered in a very few minutes.

"Look, Bill, the boat has gone!"

It was true. The grapnel, a very light one, with a short length of rope, had been thrown carelessly down on the sand when they last hauled the boat up, and as the full strength of the tide had caught the boat, it had dragged a considerable distance, and was drifting away up the Ray.

"What is to be done?" Joe exclaimed.

"Do you think we could wade along to the island, Bill?" Jack asked.

Bill shook his head. "No; there are deep channels where it would be over our heads. I can't swim a stroke, no more can Joe."

"Shall I swim to the boat, Bill, and try and get her back?"

Joe shook his head. "She is in deep water now, Jack, and the grapnel ain't holding her a bit; she will drift as fast as you can swim. But of course you can try if you like, it don't make any difference to us, for you could never beat back against this wind and tide. What fools we have been, to be sure!"

"The boats will soon be coming back now,"

Jack said hopefully. "There are some of them this side of the Chapman now."

Bill shook his head. "It will take them three quarters of an hour to beat up, Jack."

Jack turned and looked the other way. "Here are three of them coming in from the Nore, Bill. They will not be very long before they are up."

"They will be here before the others, Jack; but I doubt they will be in time. Water will be breast-high before they get up, and they may drop anchor down at the mouth of the Ray and not see us. Our best chance is the shore."

He shaded his eyes and looked steadily across at Leigh. "There is a man running from the coast-guard station," he said. "There! there are two or three others running to meet him. Now they are going back together."

The boys stood looking fixedly at the station.

"Hooray!" Jack said after a minute; "there comes the boat out of the house. Do you see they are getting her down the slip; now she is in the water." Another minute passed, and then a white sail appeared. "She is heading straight off to us, Bill. With this wind she will be here in a quarter of an hour."

But the tide was already half-way up to their

knees, and the waves beginning to splash against them.

"Will they be here in time, do you think, Bill?" Joe asked.

"I hope so, Joe," Bill said cheerily. "They would be in plenty of time if it were not for the force of the tide. Still, I think it is all right."

The minutes passed rapidly; higher and higher rose the water, and the waves increased fast in size. It was as much as the boys could do to stand against the sweep of the stream.

"Bill, you had better take Joe on your shoulders," Jack said. "I have read that one man can carry another across a stream that he couldn't get over alone."

"Jump up young un," Bill said; "and you, Jack, get off your sea-boots. You stand just behind me and hold on, I feel much steadier now that I have got Joe on my shoulders. If you feel that you are going, leave go of me, you will only pull me backward holding on; and as you can swim you are all right. You have only got to keep yourself afloat, the tide will drift you up to the island in no time."

"I don't mean to go if I can help it," Jack said. "Of course I could not swim with you two, but if you would lie on your back quiet I might manage to keep you up for a bit anyhow."

The boat, heeling far over to the breeze, was dashing along at a great pace towards them. It was a question of minutes. Jack found it extremely difficult to keep his feet, the sand seemed to be scooped out from under them by the force of the tide. The wind, which was blowing in violent gusts, added to the difficulty of withstanding the force of the current and waves.

"Don't pull, Jack," Bill said, "or you will have us over."

"I can't hold on without, Bill. Which shall I do? Swim off alone, or hold on by you till we all go together?"

"Go off by yourself, Jack; the boat will be here in five minutes now. I think I can hold on until then; anyhow, it is the best chance."

They were now waist-deep; for, little by little, as the sand gave way under their feet, they had been driven backwards towards deeper water.

"There is one other thing, Bill. Do you think you can shift Joe so as to sit on one shoulder? If I get on your other it will add to your weight."

"I will try it," Bill said; "I was nearly off my feet then. Get on to my left shoulder, Joe.

Now, Jack, you climb up. Yes, I think that is better. I should be all right if the sand would not slide away so much from under my feet."

Several times Jack felt Bill totter and sway; he was fast being swept back into the deeper water.

"If you do go, Bill, do you and Joe throw yourselves on your backs, and I will try and hold you up. The boat will be here in no time now."

She was indeed less than a hundred yards away when Bill exclaimed, "I am going!"

"Keep on your back, Bill!" Jack shouted as he went backwards under water.

The three came up close together. Jack seized the others by the hair, and throwing himself on his back, and striking out with his legs, tried to keep them in a similar position with their faces above water. Bill lay quietly enough; but Joe struggled to raise his head, and turning, grasped Jack round the body, and in a moment the three were under water.

Jack kept his presence of mind; he knew that the boat was close at hand, and strove, not to loosen the grasp of his companions, which was impossible, but to come to the surface occasionally for an instant.

Two or three times he managed this, and obtained a breath of air before he went under again. The last time, he saw the boat close at hand, and a rope fell across his face; but he could not free his hands to grasp it, and went under immediately. His senses were leaving him, when he felt something grasp him, and then knew no more till he opened his eyes, and found himself in the bottom of the boat with his two companions.

CHAPTER III.

A RUN FROM HARWICH.

ONE of the sailors, dripping wet, knelt beside him. "That is all right, lad; you will be yourself again directly."

Jack was already sufficiently recovered to sit up some time before either Bill or Joe showed signs of life; for, unable to swim or to take advantage of their momentary intervals of coming to the surface, they had become insensible some time before he had done so himself. The sailors rubbed their chests and hands, and at last both showed signs of returning animation.

"That was a close shave, Jack," the coast-guardsman who was at the helm said. "It was lucky I made you out with my glass when I did. It was touch and go; I saw you trying to get them on their backs. If they had kept quiet you would have managed it; but drowning people never will keep quiet."

They were now running up the Ray in pursuit of the boat, which had drifted into shallower water near the end of the island, and here the grapnel had brought it up. When they got up to it, the grapnel was raised and brought into the stern of the boat, and the coast-guard boat laid her course close-hauled for Leigh, towing the other behind her.

Before they arrived at the slip the other two boys were both able to sit up. They would have taken their boat up beyond the village, but one of the fishermen said, "You go home and change; you have done quite enough for to-day. Tom and I will take the boat up for you."

"That has been a lesson to me I shall not forget," Bill said as they walked along. "You saved our lives, Jack, there is not much doubt about that."

"Oh, I expect we should all have been fished out anyhow!" Jack replied.

"No, we should not, Jack. Anyhow, not alive. I thought just at first you were going to keep us up pretty easy, and then young Joe twisted round and got hold of you, and we all went down together. But I could feel then that somehow you were keeping us up, and I tried not to catch hold of your legs."

"You did not, Bill. I was able to use them just at first, and then, somehow, Joe got hold of them. However, we all kept together, that was a good thing. If we had separated, I don't suppose they would have got us all."

Fortunately the news of the danger Jack had run had not reached his mother, for she had been engaged in the back-room washing, and Lily had gone up to school.

At the first alarm many people had run down to the shore; the officer of the coast-guard with his glass had reported what was going on, and up to the last moment it had been believed that the boat would get to them in time, and there had been a gasp of dismay as he suddenly exclaimed, "They are down! The boat is only a few lengths away," he went on; "I expect they will get them. One of the men is standing up in the bow ready to jump."

A half-minute later he exclaimed, "There he goes! There, they are hoisting them into the boat!"

"Have they got them all, sir?"

"That I can't see; but I expect they have, for you see they have lowered the sail. Yes! they must have got them all, for none of them are standing up looking about, as they would be if one was missing."

Five minutes later the sail was hoisted again. The officer watched for a minute or two, and then closed his glass.

"They are going up the Ray," he said. "I expect they are going to tow the boat in here; she is under the island. They would not trouble about that unless those they have picked up were all right, but would be making straight back again to see what could be done for them."

The little crowd, now feeling that nothing worse than a ducking had happened to those on the sand, broke up and scattered to their houses. No one had known at first what boat it was whose occupants had got into trouble, and it was not till it was half-way back that it was made out to be Corbett's.

"Why, I thought he was ill in bed?" one said.

"So he is, but I expect his boys went out with it. It was not likely there was a man on board. No one but boys would be fools enough to get caught like that, and I should have thought Bill Corbett had too much sense."

"Why, Jack, what has happened?" Mrs. Robson asked as her son entered the house.

"Nothing much, mother; but we have had a ducking. There was a steamer aground on the Middle Ground, and watching her we forgot all about the tide, and the boat drifted away and we got caught. Of course I could swim, so there was no danger for me; but it would have gone hard with the two Corbetts if the sailor at the coast-guard station had not made us out, and their boat put off and picked us up."

"Well, go and change your clothes at once, Jack; it has taken all the colour out of your face. I will get a cup of hot tea ready for you by the time you come down."

It was not until some of her neighbours came in, and talked to her about the narrow escape her son had had, that Mrs. Robson realized that Jack's life had been in considerable danger, and it was well that she had him before her enjoying his tea before she learnt the truth.

"It is no use getting into a fuss about it, mother," Jack said cheerfully; "it is not going to happen again, you know. It has been a good lesson to me to keep my eyes open; and when I go cockling again I won't lose sight of the boat, not if there were twenty vessels ashore."

A few days later Jack started with his uncle

in the *Bessy* for Harwich. For himself he liked the life there better than at Leigh. At home men could not be said to live on board their boats. They went only for short trips, taking a meal before starting, and another on their return; but doing no cooking on board. Here they were out for longer hours, and the boat was always their home. They were more independent of the tide; and unless it and the wind were both dead against them, could at all times run out to their fishing ground, ten miles away, near the Cork light-ship.

The fishing was various. Soles, whiting, and haddock were the principal fish brought up in the trawls; but there was occasionally a big skate or two in the net, and these had to be handled with considerable circumspection, as they could take off a finger or two with the greatest ease with their powerful jaws and sharp teeth. These fish were always hung up in the air for a day or two before eating, as the flesh improves by keeping; the eatable portions were then cut out, and the rest was thrown overboard. These fish were for the most part eaten by the crew; the small soles, dabs, and flounders were hawked in the town, and the rest of the take sent up to London.

There was an excitement, too, in the fishing itself, apart from that connected with hauling up the trawl and examining its contents, for the sands off this coast are dangerous, and the wrecks, that have at one time or another taken place there, innumerable. Occasionally a net would catch in one of the timbers that had perhaps been lying there a hundred years or more, and then it either came up torn into fragments, or if it obtained a really firm hold, there was nothing for it but to cut the trawl-rope and lose it altogether. In fine weather, however, this step would not be taken except as a last resource. After trying in vain to get the net and trawl up the rope would be buoyed, and the next day another attempt would be made to raise the net, the boat being assisted by three or four others. The loss of a net was a serious one, as it took ten pounds or more to replace it and the trawl-beam and its belongings.

Sometimes a storm would blow up suddenly, and then the nets had to be got on board with all speed, and the topsails lowered and mainsails reefed, and the fleet of perhaps a hundred vessels would go racing back into Harwich, there to anchor just above the Guard, or under shelter of the Shotley Spit, or a short way up the Orwell, according to the direction of the wind.

The hardest part of a Leigh fisherman's life Jack had not yet encountered, for boys are seldom taken stow-boating. Stow-boating is really sprat catching, and no one can exactly explain the meaning of the term. It is carried on in winter at the edge of the sands, far down at the mouth of the river. Boats are out for many days together, frequently in terrible seas, when the boat is more under than above the water. The work of getting up the net is heavy and exhausting, and for all this hardship and labour the reward is often exceedingly slight. Sometimes the sprats are abundant, and good pay is made; sometimes, when the winter accounts are balanced up, the crew find that their share will barely suffice to pay for their keep on board, and not a farthing is left for the support of their wives and children.

Londoners who purchase sprats at an almost nominal price know but little of the hard struggle those who have caught them have to make ends meet.

After fishing for a month, Ben Tripper said one Friday evening, "We will run up to Leigh to-morrow and spend Sunday at home. I don't think we shall lose much, for the weather looks bad, and I don't think there will be any fishing to-morrow."

"I am pretty sure there won't, Ben," his mate said. "I think that it is going to blow really hard, and that we shall get wet jackets as we go up."

"We are accustomed to that," Tripper said carelessly. "Anyhow, if it comes to blow too hard for us we can make for shelter into the Crouch or Black Water."

"Oh, we are all right as to that, Ben! It is not a question of wet jackets or sea that I am thinking of, only whether we are likely to drop anchor in the Ray to-morrow night. If I were sure of that I should not mind a dusting; but I would rather lie here quiet than have a regular day's heavy knocking about, and then have to run in to Burnham after all."

"So would I," Ben assented. "If the wind comes from anywhere to the west of south it is no use thinking about it. It has been chopping and changing about to-day, and there is no saying which way it will come when it fairly makes up its mind about it; but I think from the look of the sky this evening that it is as likely to come from the north-east as not, and in that case I allow we shall make a good passage of it."

"Ay, that is right enough," Tom Hoskins assented. "They say the run from Harwich Pier to Leigh has never been done yet by a Leigh bawley under six hours, though it has been pretty close several times. We have got the springs on now, and with the wind from the north-east we should run the six hours very close, if we didn't beat it. There are two or three of them can go faster than the *Bessy* close-hauled, but running free I doubt if there is one can touch her."

"We will make a start at seven," Ben said. "We shall take the last of the ebb down to Walton, and then catch the flood and have it at its full strength by the time we are opposite Clacton."

Jack was delighted at the thought of spending a Sunday at home with his mother; but though it was not for him to give an opinion, he agreed with Tom Hoskins that they were likely to have a dusting on the way up. The sun had gone down angry and threatening; the stars could be only seen occasionally through driving masses of cloud, and even at her snug anchorage the *Bessy* was rolling heavily.

Jack was out soon after dawn. There was a haze over sea and sky, and the wind was blowing strongly; it was from the north-west now, but Jack thought that it was likely to draw round to the quarter his uncle had predicted. "There must be a heavy sea on now all the way from the Swin Middle to the Nore with the wind meeting a lee tide," he said to himself; "but of course when the ebb is done it will smooth down a bit, and will be all right if the weather does not come on too thick. A fog is bad enough and a gale is bad enough, but when you get the two together I would rather be at home and in bed by a long way than on board the *Bessy*."

"Well, Jack, what do you make out of the weather?" Ben Tripper asked, as he came out from the fo'castle.

"It looks rather wild, uncle; but I think the wind is working round to the north of east, just as you thought it would last night."

"Yes; I think it is," Ben said, surveying the sky. "Well, get the fire alight at once, Jack, and get breakfast ready; we will have our meal before we start. We shall have enough to do when we are once under way. I will run down to the Naze anyhow, and then we shall see what it is like outside. If we don't like its looks we can pop back anyhow; and shall have lost nothing, for there is no shooting nets to-day, that is quite certain."

The topmast was lowered, small jib and foresail got up, and two reefs put in the mainsail; then they began to get up the anchor.

"What! are you going up home, Tripper?" shouted a man from the next boat.

"Ay, ay, lad!"

"You will get your decks washed before you get to the Mouse!"

"Do them good and save us trouble!" Tripper shouted back.

"Tell the missis if you see her she may expect to see me next Saturday if the wind is right." Tripper threw up his arm to show he understood, and then lent his aid in getting up the anchor.

"Put up the helm, Jack; the anchor is free. That is enough. Keep her jib just full and no more till we have stowed all away here." When the chain was stowed below, and the anchor securely fastened, Tripper went aft and hauled in the main-sheet. "Up with the foresail, Tom. That is it. You keep the tiller, Jack." The two men now proceeded to coil down all the ropes, and get everything ship-shape and tidy. By the time they had finished, Harwich was fairly behind them, and they were lying their course a point or two outside the Naze, throwing the spray high each time the boat plunged into the short choppy sea.

"Nice place this, Jack," his uncle said. "There is always a sea on the shallows if the wind is anywhere against tide. No wonder they call it the Rolling Ground. There, I will take the helm now. You had best get the compass up; I can't make out the point sometimes through the mist."

An hour and a quarter from the time of getting up the anchor the *Bessy* was off the point. As soon as the ugly ledge of rocks running far out under water was weathered, Tripper put down the helm.

"Haul in the sheet, Tom. That is right; now the sail is over. Slack out—slack out all it will go; the wind is nearly dead aft. Ease off the jib-sheet, Jack. That is it. Now she is walking along."

The motion was smooth and easy now. The waves were much higher than in the shelter of the bay, but they were running easily and regularly, in nearly the same line the boat was following. Coming up threateningly behind her, they lifted the stern high into the air, passing gently under her, hurrying her along as she was on the crest, and then passing on ahead and dropping her gently down into the hollow.

"I think she would stand a reef shaken out, uncle," Jack said.

"She has got quite enough on her, Jack, and is walking along at a grand pace. Always leave well alone, lad. The squalls come up very strong sometimes, and I would not carry as much sail as we have got if she were a cutter with a heavy boom. As it is, we can brail it up at any moment if need be. We sha'n't be long getting down off Clacton. Then you must keep a sharp look-out for the Spitway Buoy. It comes on very thick at times, and it is difficult to judge how far we are out. However, I think I know pretty well the direction it lies in, and can hit it to within a cable's length or so. I have found it many a time on a dark night, and am not likely to miss it now. It will take us an hour and a half or so from the time we pass Walton till we are up to the buoy.

CHAPTER IV.

THE WRECK.

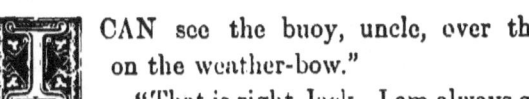 CAN see the buoy, uncle, over there on the weather-bow."

"That is right, Jack. I am always glad when we get that buoy; it is the hardest to find of any of them. We shall have to jibe going round it. You stand by to brail the sail up when I give the word; we might carry away the gaff at the jaws if we let the sail go over all standing now." As soon as they neared the buoy Tom Hoskins got in the oar with which the mainsail was boomed out. "Now, Jack, brail up the sail as she comes round. Haul in the sheet as fast as you can, Tom, and pay it out again handsomely as it comes over. That is the way. Now fasten the sheet and throw off the main-tack and trice the sail up pretty near to the throat.

"That will do. Slack the brail off, Jack. Now haul in the sheet a bit. You had better let the foresail down, Tom; the wind is heavy, and there is too much sea on here to drive her through it too fast."

The sea would have been far heavier than it now was in another two hours' time, but the water was still very shallow on the sands, and this broke the force of the waves. The boat was now running along the narrow channel of deep water leading between the Spitway Buoy and the Bell Buoy, and almost at right angles to the course they had before been following. The wind was almost on their beam, and even under the reduced canvas the *Bessy* was lying far over, the water covering three planks of her deck on the starboard side. They could see the buoy, and presently could hear its deep tolling as the hammers struck the bell with every motion of the buoy.

"Ah! here is another heavy rain squall coming down. I am glad we are round the Bell Buoy before it came up. Jack, you may as well put the tea-kettle on. A cup of tea will be a comfort."

All three were wrapped up in oil-skins; but in spite of this they had a general sensation of dampness, for it had been raining more or less ever since they started. Jack was below, when he heard a far louder roar of the wind than before, and heard his uncle shout, "Brail up the main as far as you can, Tom—the jib is about all we want now!"

Jack looked out from the fo'castle. The wind was blowing tremendously, sweeping the heads off the waves and driving them into sheets of spray; then great drops of rain struck the deck almost with the force of bullets, and a minute later it came down almost in bucketfuls.

"Do you want me, uncle?" he shouted. His voice did not reach Ben's ears, but he guessed what he had said and waved his hand to him to remain in the fo'castle. Jack took off his sou'-wester and shook the water from his oil-skin, and then opening the locker where the coke was kept replenished the fire. It settled down so dark when the squall struck the boat that he could scarce see across the little cabin. Regardless of the howling of the wind and the motion of the vessel, he sat on the floor putting in stick after stick to hasten up the fire. As soon as the kettle boiled he put in a handful of tea and some sugar and took the kettle off the fire, then he got a couple of large mugs and half-filled them with tea, and sat balancing them until the fluid was sufficiently cool to be drunk. Then tying on his sou'-

wester again he made his way out and gave a mug to each of the others.

"Go down below again, Jack!" his uncle shouted at the top of his voice, and although Jack was within two or three feet of him, he scarcely heard him. "There is nothing to be done at present here, and it is no use looking out for the Swin Middle at present."

Jack took a look round before he went below. Away at some distance on either hand were white masses of foam where the sea was breaking on the sands. He went up to the bow and looked ahead through the darkness, then he went back to his uncle. "I caught sight of a light right over the bowsprit."

"Ah! they have lit up then," Tripper said. "I thought they would, for it is almost as dark as night. You had best get the side-lights ready and the flare-up. I don't suppose we shall want them, for if we see a steamer coming down we will give her a clear berth. They won't be able to look far ahead in the face of this wind and rain." Jack went forward again and lay down on the lockers. He thought little of the storm. It was a severe one, no doubt, but with the wind nearly due aft, and a weather tide, it was nothing to the *Bessy*, whose great beam in comparison to her length enabled her to run easily before the wind, when a long narrow craft would have been burying herself.

Presently he thought he heard his uncle shout, and getting up looked aft. Tom Hoskins was now at the helm. Tripper was standing beside him, and pointing at something broad away on the beam. Jack at once made his way aft.

"What is it, uncle?"

"I saw the flash of a gun. Ah! there it is again. There is a ship ashore on the Middle Sunk." Jack gazed in the direction in which his uncle was pointing. In a minute there was another flash.

"It is all over with her," Ben Tripper said solemnly. "The strongest ship that ever was built could not hold together long on that sand with such a sea on as there will be there now."

"Cannot we do something?"

"Tripper was silent for half a minute. "What do you think, Tom? We might get there through the swashway. There is plenty of water for us, and we could lay our course there. It is a risky business, you know, and we may not be able to get near her when we get there; but that we cannot tell till we see how she is fixed. Still, if we could get there before she goes to pieces we might perhaps save some of them."

"I don't mind, Ben, if you don't," the other said "I have neither wife nor child, and if you like to take the risk, I am ready."

Ben Tripper looked at Jack. "I would not mind if it wasn't for the boy," he said.

"Don't mind me, uncle," Jack burst out. "I would not have you hang back because of me, not for anything in the world. Do try it, uncle. It would be awful to think of afterwards, when we hear of her being lost with all hands, that we might have saved some of them perhaps if we had tried."

Ben still hesitated, when another bright flash was seen. It was an appeal for aid he could not resist. "Put down the helm, Tom," he said. "Now, Jack, help me to rouse in the sheet. That will do. Now then for a pull on the jib-sheet. Now we will put the last reef in the foresail and hoist it, slack the brail and haul down the maintack a bit. We must keep good way on her crossing the tide." Now that they were nearly close-hauled instead of running before the wind, Jack recognized much more strongly than before how heavy was the sea and how great the force of the wind. Lively as the boat was, great masses of water poured over her bow and swept aft as each wave struck her. Her lee bulwarks were completely buried.

"Give me the helm, Tom," Tripper said; "and get those hatchways up and cover the well, and lash the tarpaulin over it. It is bad enough here, it will be worse when we get into broken water near the wreck." Most of the bawleys are provided with hatches for closing the long narrow place known as the 'well,' but it is only under quite exceptional circumstances that they are ever used. Jack and the man got them up and managed to fit them in their places, but getting the tarpaulin over them was beyond their power.

"I will throw her up into the wind," Ben said. "Haul on the weather fore-sheet as I do, and belay it with the foot of the sail just to windward of the mast. Now rouse in the main-sheet. That is right."

Quitting the tiller as the boat lay-to to the wind, Ben lent his aid to the other two, and in three or four minutes the tarpaulin was securely lashed over the hatches, and the boat completely battened down.

"Now, Jack, you had best lash yourself to something or you will be swept overboard; we shall have it a lot worse than this presently. Now, Tom, before we get well away again get the last reef in the mainsail, then we can haul the tack down taut again; the sail will stand much better so, and we shall want to keep her all to windward if she is to go through the swashway."

When all was ready the fore weather-sheet was let go, and the lee-sheet hauled taut. The mainsheet was slacked off a little and the *Bessy* proceeded on her way. It was a terrible half-hour; fortunately the dense heavy clouds had broken a little, and it was lighter than it had been, but this only rendered the danger more distinct. Once in the swashway, which is the name given to a narrow channel between the sands, the waves were less high. But on either hand they were breaking wildly, for there were still but four or five feet of water over the sands. The sea was nearly abeam now, and several times Jack almost held his breath as the waves lifted the *Bessy* bodily to leeward and threatened to cast her into the breaking waters but a few fathoms away. But the skipper knew his boat well and humoured her through the waves, taking advantage of every squall to eat up a little to windward, but always keeping her sails full and plenty of way on her. At last they were through the swashway; and though the sea was again heavier, and the waves frequently swept over the decks, Jack gave a sigh of relief. They could make out the hull of the vessel now looming up black over the white surf that surrounded it. She had ceased firing, either from the powder being wetted or her guns disabled.

"Which way had we better get at her, Tom?" Ben Tripper asked. "She is pretty near on the top of the sand."

"The only way we have a chance of helping her is by laying-to, or anchoring on the edge of the sand to leeward of her. They may be able to drift a line down to us. I do not see any other way. Our anchors wouldn't hold to windward of her."

"No; I suppose that is the best way, Tom. We must make the best allowance we can for the wind and the set of tide, otherwise they will never drift a line down to us. She won't hold together long. Her stern is gone as far as the mizzen, so we must be quick about it."

The wreck was evidently a sailing vessel. Her masts were all gone, her bulwarks carried away, and she lay far heeled over. A group of people could be seen huddled up in the bow as they neared her. Tom Hoskins and Jack had for the last ten minutes been busy getting the spare anchor up on deck and fastening to it the warp of the trawl-net, which was by far the strongest rope they had on board.

"What water is there on the sand, Ben?"

"Six or seven feet on the edge, but less further on. We do not draw over five feet, so we will keep on till we touch. The moment we do so let the two anchors go. Wind and tide will take her off again quick enough. Pay out ten or twelve fathoms of chain, and directly she holds up drop the lead-line overboard to see if she drags; if she does, give her some more rope and chain."

The anchors were both got overboard and in readiness to let go at a moment's notice, the instant the *Bessy* took ground.

The foresail was lowered and the mainsail partly brailed up, so that she had only way on her sufficient to stem the tide. As they entered the broken water Jack was obliged to take a step back and hold on to the mast. Her motion had before been violent, but to a certain extent regular; now she was tossed in all directions so sharply and violently that he expected every moment that the mast would go. Tom looked round at Ben. The latter pointed to the sail and waved his hand. Tom understood him, and going to the mast loosened the brail a little to give her more sail, for the waves completely knocked the way out of her. When she forged ahead again, Tom returned to his post.

Jack held his breath every time the boat pitched, but she kept on without touching until within some eighty yards of the wreck; then as she pitched forward down a wave there was a shock that nearly threw Jack off his feet, prepared for it though he was. In a moment he steadied himself, and crept forward and cut the lashing of the hawser just as Tom severed that of the chain. The latter rattled out for a moment. There was another shock, but less violent than the first, and then the renewed rattle of the chain showed that she was drifting astern. Ben now left the tiller and sprang forward. The jib was run in by the traveller and got down, the foresail had been cast off and had run down the forestay the moment she struck, and the three now set to work to lower the mainsail.

"She is dragging," Tom said, examining the lead-line, "but not fast."

"Give her another five or six fathoms of chain," Ben said, himself attending to the veering out of the hawser.

This done they again watched the lead-line. It hung straight down by the side of the vessel.

"They have got her," Ben said. "Now then for the ship."

For the first time since they entered the broken water they had leisure to look about them. Those on board the ship had lost no time, and had already launched a light spar with a line tied to it into the water.

"It will miss us," Ben said, after watching the spar for a minute. "You see, I allowed for wind and tide, and the wind does not affect the spar, and the tide will sweep it down thirty or forty yards on our port bow."

It turned out so. Those on board payed out the line until the spar floated abreast of the smack, but at a distance of some thirty yards away.

"What is to be done?" Ben asked. "If we were to try to get up sail again we should drift away so far to leeward we should never be able to beat back."

"Look here," Jack said; "if you signal to them to veer out some more rope I could soon do it.

I could not swim across the tide now, but if it were twenty fathom further astern I could manage it."

" You could never swim in that sea, Jack."

" Well, I could try, uncle. Of course you would fasten a line round me, and if I cannot get there you will haul me in again. There cannot be any danger about that."

So saying Jack at once proceeded to throw off his oil-skins and sea-boots, while Ben went to the bow of the boat and waved to those on the wreck to slack out more line. They soon understood him, and the spar was presently floating twenty yards further astern. Jack had by this time stripped. A strong line was now fastened round his body under his arms, and going up to the bow of the boat, so as to give himself as long a distance as possible to drift, he prepared for the swim.

CHAPTER V.

THE RESCUE.

J ACK was a good swimmer, but he had never swum in a sea like this.

"If I raise my arms, uncle, pull in at once. If I see I cannot reach the spar I sha'n't exhaust myself by going on, but shall come back and take a fresh start. Let me have plenty of rope."

"All right, Jack! we won't check you."

Jack took a header, and swimming hard under water came up some distance from the boat.

"He will do it," Tom shouted in Ben's ear. "He is nigh half-way between this and the rope already."

It was, however, a more difficult task than it looked. Had the water been smooth it would have been easy for Jack to swim across the tide to the spar before he was swept below it, but he found at once that it was impossible to swim fast, so buffeted and tossed was he by the sea, while he was almost smothered by the spray carried by the wind to the top of the waves. He trod water for a moment with his back to the wind, took a deep breath, and then dived again. When he came up he was delighted to see that he was as near as possible in the line of the spar, which was towing but a few yards from him. He ceased swimming, and a moment later the tide swept him down upon it.

He had before starting fastened a piece of lashing three feet long to the loop round his chest, and the moment he reached the spar he lashed this firmly round the rope, and passing one arm round the spar lifted the other above his head. In a moment he felt the strain of the rope round his chest, and this soon tightened above the water. But Jack felt that the strain of pulling not only him but the spar through the water might be too much for it, and rather than run the risk he again waved his hand, and as soon as the line slacked he fastened it to the rope from the wreck, loosened the hitches round the spar and allowed the latter to float away. He was half drowned by the time he reached the side of the hawley, for he had been dragged in the teeth of the wind and tide, and each wave had swept clean over his head.

At first those on board pulled but slowly, in

order to enable him to swim over the top of the waves. But the force of the spray in his face was so great that he could not breathe, and he waved to them that they must draw him in at once. As soon as they understood him they pulled in the rope with a will, and more under than above the water he was brought to the side of the smack and lifted on board, the wind bringing down the sound of a cheer from those on board the wreck as he was got out of the water. Ben undid the line round his body, carried him downstairs, wrapped a couple of blankets round him and laid him down on the lockers, and then ran upstairs to assist Tom, who had carried the line forward and was already hauling it in.

"That is right, Tom. They have got a good strong hawser on it, I see, and there is a light line coming with it to carry the slings."

As soon as the end of the hawser came on board it was fastened to the mast. The line by which it had been hauled in was unfastened and tied to that looped round the hawser, and payed out as those on the deck hauled on it. A minute later two sailors got over the bulwarks, and a woman was lifted over to them and placed in the strong sling beneath the hawser. A lashing was put round her, and then they waved their hands and the fishermen hauled on the line. In two minutes the woman was on the deck of the smack; the lashing was unfastened and knotted on to the sling ready for the next passenger, then at Ben's signal that all was ready those on board the wreck hauled the sling back again.

Jack remained between the blankets for a minute or two. He had not lost consciousness; and as soon as his breath came he jumped up, gave himself a rub with the blanket, slipped into some dry clothes, and was on deck just as the woman arrived. She was all but insensible, and directly the sling had started on its return journey Ben carried her on into the fo'castle.

"Jack! set to work and make a lot of cocoa. There are no spirits on board; but cocoa is better, after all. Put the other kettle on and chuck plenty of wood upon the fire, and as soon as the one that is boiling now is empty, fill that up again. I should say there are twenty or thirty of them, and a pint apiece will not be too much. Take a drink yourself, lad, as soon as you have made it. You want it as much as they do."

Fast the shipwrecked people came along the line. There was not a moment to lose, for the wreck was breaking up fast, and every sea brought floating timbers past the bawley.

"It is a good job now, Tom, that we anchored where we did, instead of in the direct line of the tide, for one of those timbers would stave a hole in her bow as if she were a bandbox."

"Aye, that it would, Ben. I thought we had made rather a mess of it at first; but it is well that, as you say, we ain't in the line of the drift."

Nineteen persons were brought on board—the captain being the last to come along the line. The first four were women, or rather, the first two were women; the third a girl of ten years old, and the fourth a woman. Then came a middle-aged man, evidently a passenger. Then came ten sailors, a steward, two mates, and the captain.

"Is that all?" Ben asked, as the captain stepped from the slings.

"I am the last," the captain said. "Thank God all are saved who were left on board when you came in sight. We all owe our lives to you and your men. I had little hope that one of us would live to see the night when we made you out coming towards us. But there is no time to talk. The ship cannot hold together many minutes longer, and when she breaks up in earnest some of the timbers will be sure to come this way."

"I have got the buoy with a length of rope on the chain ready to slip," Ben said, "and a spar lashed to the hawser. Now, Tom, let the chain out; I will jump below and knock out the shackle. Now, captain, if one or two of your men will lend us a hand to get up some canvas, we shall be out of it all the sooner. And please get them all except the women out of the cabin, and put them aft. We want her head well up for running before this sea."

"Now, lads, tumble out and lend a hand," the captain said. "I see you have got some cocoa here. Well, all who have had a mug come out at once, and let the others get aft as soon as they have had their share. The ladies are all right, I hope?"

"Quite right, captain," one of the men answered, "and begin to feel warm already; which is natural enough, for this cabin is like an oven after the deck of the *Petrel*."

"Now, skipper, do you give the orders," the captain said as Ben took the tiller.

"Run up the foresail and haul in the starboard-sheet. That will bring her head round."

"Now let go the cable and hawser." There was a sharp rattle of chains, and the cry "All free!"

"Slack off that weather-sheet and haul down on the lee-sheet," was Tripper's next order. "Not too much. Have you got the jib hooked on to the traveller? Out with it, then. Now, up with her. Now man the throat and peak halliards. Up with her. Slack out the main-sheet well, and boom the sail out with an oar. Trice the main-tack up as far as it will go."

The *Bessy* was now running almost before the wind. Every moment the great waves loomed up high behind her stern, and looked as if they would dash down upon her deck, but she slipped easily away. The clouds had broken up much now, but the wind had in no way abated. A gleam or two of sunlight made its way through the rifts of the clouds, and threw light green patches upon the gray and angry sea.

"She is a splendid sea-boat this of yours," the captain said. "I would hardly have believed such a small craft would have made such good weather in such a sea."

"There are few boats will beat a bawley," Ben said. "Well handled, they will live through pretty near anything."

"I can quite believe that. Which of you was it who sprang overboard to get our line?"

"It was not either of us," Ben said. "Neither Tom nor I can swim a stroke. It was my nephew Jack—that lad who has just come out of the forecastle."

"It was a gallant action," the captain said. "I should have thought it well-nigh impossible to swim in such broken water. I was astonished when I saw him leap overboard."

"He saw that the spar had drifted with the tide to windward of you and there was no other way of getting at it."

"I was in hopes of seeing you throw the lead-line over our line. You might have hauled it in that way."

"So we might," Ben agreed, "if we had thought of it, though I doubt whether we could have cast it so far. Still we ought to have tried. That was a stupid trick, to be sure. I allow I should have thought of it any other time; but we had had such a dusting in getting up to you that our brains must have gone wool-gathering."

"One cannot think of everything," the captain said. "You had your hands full as it was. Is there anything else I can do at present? If not,

I will just go below for a minute and see how my wife and the passengers are getting on, and have a cup of that cocoa, if there is any left."

They were now in the Knob Channel, and the sea, although still heavy, was more regular. As they passed the Mouse Light-ship there were several large steamers at anchor there, but it was now a straight run down to the Nore and they held on.

Ben Tripper had already asked the captain where he would like to be landed. "I can put you either into Sheerness, Southend, or Leigh," he said. "Tide is high now, and you can land at any of them without difficulty. But you would get more quickly up to town from Southend or Leigh; and I should recommend our side, because tide will be running out from the Medway pretty strong before we get there, and when that is the case there is a nasty sea at the mouth."

"I think we cannot do better than Leigh," the captain said. "Of course I am anxious to get on shore as soon as I can to get the women into dry clothes."

"It will not make more than twenty minutes' difference whether you land at Leigh or Southend; and it is much handier for landing at Leigh, and no distance to the inn, where they can get between blankets while their things are being dried."

"Then Leigh let it be. A few minutes will make no difference one way or the other, and if they have not caught cold already they will not do so in that warm cabin."

The wind was blowing far too strongly to admit of conversation, except in shouted sentences. Fortunately there was a good supply of tobacco on board, and the rescued sailors, who had almost all a pipe in their pockets, had, after the smack was once clear of the broken water, enjoyed the consolation of a smoke.

Accustomed to look down on the water from the high deck of a large ship, they had at first felt some doubt as to the ability of the low bawley to struggle safely through the towering waves; but as soon as they saw how well she behaved, and how little water she took over the sides, they felt that all danger was over, and became disposed to look at things more cheerfully.

The steward had, as soon as he came on board, relieved Jack of his duties at the galley, and had kept the kettles going; he now served out a second supply of cocoa all round, and hung up as many of the ladies' things as they could dispense with round the fire to dry.

The passenger had remained below with the ladies. He was suffering from a broken leg, having been knocked down and swept along by the sea soon after the vessel struck. Six of the sailors and two of the mates had either been washed overboard or crushed to death when the masts went over the side.

As they passed the Nore a perfect fleet of steamers and sailing-vessels were at anchor there. Tide had turned strongly now, and there was a nasty heavy choppy sea until the *Bessy* passed the end of Southend Pier, when she entered comparatively smooth water. In less than half an hour the sails were lowered, and she anchored some fifty yards from the coast-guard station.

The look-out there had already observed the number of people on her deck, and had guessed at once that she had taken the crew off a wreck of some kind, and as soon as the anchor was dropped their boat came alongside.

The captain had as they neared the shore asked Tripper about inns, and at once sent the crew ashore in charge of the mate, with orders to go to the "Bell;" and to see that they had everything they required, saying that he would himself, as soon as the ladies were on shore, go to one of the shops and order a supply of clothes to be sent up for them.

The ladies were next taken ashore, and then the injured man carried up and placed in a boat, a stretcher being sent off for him to be laid on. A messenger had been already sent up to the doctor on the top of the hill to come down to the Ship Inn, where the party now went. The ladies had become so thoroughly warmed by the heat in the little cabin that they declined to go to bed, and having been supplied with dry garments by the landlady, they were soon comfortable.

The surgeon on his arrival pronounced the fracture of the passenger's leg, which was a few inches above the ankle, to be a simple one, and not likely to be attended with any serious consequences whatever. After setting it he bandaged it in splints, and said that although he should recommend a few days' perfect quiet, there was no actual reason why the patient should not be taken up to London if he particularly wished it.

Ben Tripper had gone with the captain, and a pile of flannel shirts, stockings, guernseys, trou-

sers, and shoes had at once been sent up to the
"Bell." Furious as was the gale, it was possible
to speak so as to be heard in the street of Leigh,
and Ben now learned for the first time some particulars about the wreck.

"The *Petrel* was a seven hundred ton ship,"
the captain said, "and on her way home from
Australia. She belongs to James Godstone & Son.
There is no James Godstone now. The son is the
passenger you saved; he is the owner of a dozen
vessels all about the same size as the *Petrel*. His
wife and daughter are two of the ladies saved.
They went out with us to Australia. The girl was
not strong, and had been recommended a sea
voyage.

"I had been married when I was at home last
time, and was taking my wife out with me; so
Mr. Godstone arranged that his wife and daughter
should go with me. We carried no other passengers; the other woman saved is the stewardess.
Mr. Godstone himself did not go out with us, but
went across by Suez and joined us there for the
homeward voyage. We made a fine run home;
and took our pilot on board off Deal. The gale
was blowing up then; but as it looked as if it was
coming from the north-east we did not care about

riding it out in the Downs, or going back so as to be under shelter of the South Foreland.

"It did not come on really heavy till we were nearly off Margate, and then we got it with a vengeance. Still, as the wind was free, we kept on. Then, as you know, it came on almost pitch dark, and I think the pilot lost his head. Anyhow, as he was one of those who were drowned, we need not say whether he was to blame or not. I thought we were getting too close to the broken water, and told him so, but he said we were all right. He didn't make allowance enough, I think, for the leeway she was making, and a minute later she struck, and you can guess the rest. Her back broke in a few minutes, and her mizzen went over the side, carrying with it the pilot, my first mate, and six sailors.

"She soon after began to break up at the stern. I cut away the other two masts to relieve her, but the sea made a clear breach over her. I got the ladies and Mr. Godstone, who had been on deck when she struck and got his leg broken by the first sea which pooped her, forward as soon as I could, and managed to fire one of her guns three times. I had no hope of rescue coming from shore, but there was a chance of some ship coming up helping us; though how she was to do it I could not see. However, nothing came near until I saw your sail. I expect that any steamers coming up from the south brought up under the Foreland, while those from the north would of course take the Swin. Anyhow, it would have been all over with us had you not come to our rescue. Even when I saw you making over towards us I had not much hope, for I did not see how you could get close enough to us to aid us, and I was quite sure that no open boat could have lived in that broken water."

CHAPTER VI.

ALTERED PROSPECTS.

AS soon as the shipwrecked crew were on shore, Jack Robson landed and made his way homeward. At the railway-crossing he met his mother hurrying down, for the news that the *Bessy* had arrived with a number of shipwrecked people had spread rapidly through the place.

"Well, Jack, so I hear the *Bessy* has been helping a wreck. I had no idea that you would be home to-day. What in the world induced your uncle to make the run in such weather as this?"

"It was nothing like so bad when we started, mother, and as we had both wind and tide with us there was nothing to fear for the *Bessy*. We are accustomed to wet jackets, and should have got nothing worse if it had not been for our hearing guns and making for the wreck. Then we certainly had a tremendous sea, the heaviest I have ever been out in. However, we were under storm-sails and did very well. It was nasty work when we anchored in broken water near the wreck, and she jumped about so I thought the mast would have gone. However, everything held, and we managed to save nineteen people from the wreck. That is a pleasant thought, mother, and I would go through it again twenty times to do it." By this time they had reached the door of the house.

"There, run upstairs and change, Jack. I will get you some tea ready by the time you come down."

"I have had some hot cocoa, mother, and am as right as possible. Still, I shall not object to a cup of tea and something to eat with it. We had breakfast before we started at eight, and it is seven now. We thought when we hoisted sail we should be down here under the six hours, but of course going off to the wreck made all the difference. And, anyhow, we could not have driven her fast in such a sea."

By the time Jack had had his tea a comfortable glow had come over him. Now that it was all over he felt bruised and stiff from the buffeting he had gone through, and after half an hour's chat with his mother and sister, in which he told them more fully the events of the wreck, he turned into bed and slept soundly till the morning. Captain Murchison, for that was his name, came round half an hour after Jack had gone up to bed to ask him to go round to the inn, as the ladies wished to see him and thank him for his share in rescuing them, but on hearing that he had gone up to bed asked his mother to request him to come round in the morning at ten o'clock.

"You have reason to be proud of your son, Mrs. Robson," he said. "His leaping over in such a sea as that to get hold of the line from our ship was a most gallant action."

"He told me the line was tied round him, sir, so that there was no danger in it at all."

"There is always danger in such a business as that, Mrs. Robson. The force of the waves in shallow water is tremendous, and will beat a man to death if they do not drown him. Then there is the difficulty of his getting on board again when a vessel is rolling and pitching so tremendously, and the danger of his being struck by a piece of drift-wood from the wreck. I can assure you that it was a very grand action, whatever your son may have told you about it."

The next morning the gale was still blowing

fiercely, although with less strength than on the previous day. Jack had heard from his mother of his appointment to go to the "Ship" with much discontent, and had at first positively refused to go.

"I hate going up to see strange people, mother, anyhow; and I am sure that I do not want to be thanked. I am glad enough to have had a share in saving all their lives, but of course it was all Uncle Ben and Tom's handling the boat that did it; I had nothing to do with it whatever, except that little swim with the rope tied safely round me. Why, it was nothing to that affair that I had with Bill and Joe Corbett."

"But you must go, Jack; the ladies naturally wish to thank you for what you did for them, and whether you like it or not you must go. It would be very rude and uncivil not to do so. They would be sure to send round here if you did not come, and what should I say except that you were so unmannerly that you would not go."

Jack twisted himself on his chair uncomfortably.

"I don't see why they shouldn't thank Uncle Ben for the lot and have done with it," he grumbled. "It is his boat and he was the skipper, and he did it all; besides, I expect the *Bessy* will have to be overhauled before she goes out again. She came down with a tremendous crash on her forefoot, and the water was just coming up through the boards in the fo'castle when we came in. Of course it may have come in from above, but I expect she sprang a leak somewhere forward. I thought she was very low in the water when she came in, and I expect that she must have been half full aft, for she was very much down by the stern.

"We had the pump going all the time, and it was always clear water. I did not think of it at the time. We had had such a lot of water over us it was likely it might have got in through the hatches; but I feel sure now that it was a leak. Well, I suppose if I must go, I must, mother; but I hate it for all that."

However, just before Jack was about to start there was a knock at the door, and Mrs. Robson opening it saw two ladies and a girl. Immediately on their arrival the evening before, Mrs. Godstone had telegraphed home for a servant to come down in the morning by the first train, with clothes for herself and daughter, and she had arrived with them an hour before. Mrs. Godstone had therefore been enabled to resume her usual attire, and to lend an outfit to Mrs. Murchison. Jack did not in the least recognize in the three ladies the soaked and draggled women, of whose faces he had caught but a slight glimpse on the previous day.

"We have come round, Mrs. Robson," Mrs. Godstone began, "to thank your son for his share in saving our lives yesterday. We thought that it would be more pleasant to him than coming round to us at the inn."

"Thank you, madam," Mrs. Robson replied. "It was kind of you to think of it. I have had a good deal of trouble in persuading Jack to go round. He was just starting; but it was very much against the grain, I can assure you. Come in, please."

Mrs. Godstone was surprised at the tone in which this fisher lad's mother spoke, for during her thirteen years of married life Bessy Robson had lost the Essex dialect, and acquired the manners of her husband's friends. She was still more surprised at the pretty furniture of the room, which was tastefully decorated, and the walls hung with pictures of marine subjects, for Bessy had brought down bodily her belongings from

Dulwich. Mrs. Godstone at once walked up to Jack with outstretched hand.

"I hope you are none the worse for your exertions of yesterday," she said. "My daughter and I have come round to thank you for the very great service you rendered us."

Mrs. Murchison and Mildred Godstone also shook hands with Jack. The former added her thanks to Mrs. Godstone's.

Jack coloured up hotly and said, "It is my uncle you have to thank, ma'am. It was his bawley, and he and Tom sailed it, and I had nothing to do with it one way or the other."

"Except when you swam out for the line," Mrs. Godstone said smiling.

"I had one tied round me, and was all right," Jack protested.

"My husband does not think it was nothing, as you seem to consider," Mrs Murchison said; "and as he has been a sailor all his life he ought to know. He says that it was a very gallant action in such a sea as that, and, you see, we are bound to believe him."

The ladies had now taken seats. Mrs. Godstone felt a little at a loss. Had Jack's home and Jack's mother been what they had expected to find them the matter would have been simple enough, but she felt at once that any talk of reward for the service Jack had rendered them would be at present impossible.

"What a pretty room you have got, Mrs. Robson, and what charming pictures!"

"They are my husband's painting," Mrs. Robson said quietly. "He was an artist."

"Oh! I know the name," Mrs. Godstone said. "I have four of Mr. Robson's pictures in my drawing-room. I am very fond of marine subjects."

This served as an introduction, and for half an hour the conversation proceeded briskly. Then Mrs. Godstone rose.

"My husband's leg is very painful this morning," she said, "and I fear that he will have to keep his bed for the next two or three days. When he is well enough to lie down on the sofa I will come down and fetch your son, for Mr. Godstone is of course anxious to see him, and I am afraid that if I do not come round myself we shall not get Jack to the inn."

"Well, that was not so very bad, was it, Jack?" Mrs. Robson asked after her visitors had left.

"No, mother, it wasn't. You see, it was ever

so much better their coming here than it would have been if I had gone to the inn, because there was you for them to talk to, so that really there was not much said to me. If it had been at the inn there would have been nothing to talk about at all, except about the wreck. Well, now that is over I will go down and see how the bawley is; but I had best change my things first. Uncle was going to get her up as high as he could at the top of the tide, so as to be able to look at her keel."

Jack found that his uncle and Tom had turned out at three o'clock in the morning, and had got the *Bessy* as high up as possible on the sloping shore, just beyond the houses. They were standing beside her now, while Benting, the local boat-builder, was examining her bottom.

"Well, Jack, you have taken it out in sleep this morning," his uncle said.

"That I have, uncle. I never woke until eight o'clock, so I had just twelve hours' sleep."

"Nothing like a good sleep, Jack, when you have had a hard day's work; and yesterday was enough to take it out of anyone."

"Is she damaged at all?" Jack asked.

"Yes, her forefoot is sprung just where it joins the keel; she came down just on the joint."

"That will be a rather nasty job to get right, won't it?"

"Yes, Jack, Benting says she must have a new stem altogether. He does not think the keel is damaged, but the stem is cracked right through."

"That will cost a lot, won't it?" Jack said.

"Yes, it is a nasty job, Jack; because, of course, she will want a lot of fresh planks in her. In fact, she will want pretty well rebuilding forward of the mast."

"It will cost about twenty pounds to make a good job of it," Benting said as he joined them. "I shouldn't like to take the job for less, not on contract. If I did day-work it might come to a little less or a little more, I cannot say."

Jack looked anxiously up into his uncle's face, for he knew that twenty pounds was a serious matter.

"It won't be at my expense, Jack," Ben replied to his look. "Captain Murchison came down at seven o'clock this morning and had a look at her with me. I told him yesterday that I was afraid she had damaged herself on the sand, as she had made a lot of water on her way up. He said that I was to have her examined at once and get an estimate for repairing her thoroughly, and that he would undertake it should be paid. He asked

**IMAGE EVALUATION
TEST TARGET (MT-3)**

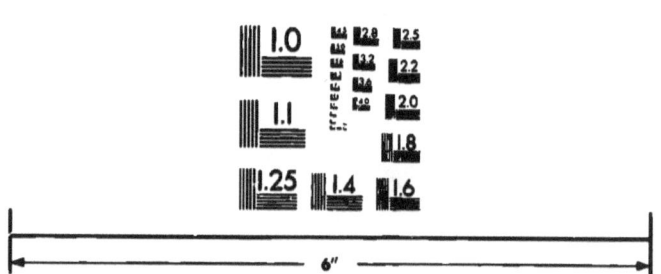

6"

Photographic
Sciences
Corporation

23 WEST MAIN STREET
WEBSTER, N.Y. 14580
(716) 872-4503

what her age was. Of course I told him she was only four years old, and that I had only finished paying off the money I borrowed when I had her built, last year. He said that as she was only four years old she was worth spending the money on; but if she had been an old boat, it would not have been worth while throwing money away on her. But Benting says he can make her as good as new again."

"Every bit," the carpenter said. "She will be just as strong as she was on the day she was turned out."

"How long will you be about it?"

"I would get her done in three weeks. I will go over to Southend by the twelve o'clock train and order the timber, and you can arrange this evening whether you will have her done by contract or day-work."

Captain Murchison that evening when he returned from town, where he had gone up to report to Lloyd's the loss of the ship, had a talk with Benting, and being assured by him that the *Bessy* would after the execution of the repairs be in all respects as stout a craft as before, arranged with him to do it for the sum he named, and to set to work immediately.

Three days later Mr. Godstone was able to be brought out on to the sofa in the sitting-room. Captain and Mrs. Murchison had gone home two days before, but the former came down again to Leigh on the morning Mr. Godstone got up. After a talk together Captain Murchison went out and fetched Ben Tripper in, and Mr. Godstone presented him with a cheque for a hundred pounds for himself and fifty for Tom Hoskins.

"We owe you our lives," he said, "and we shall never forget the service you have rendered us. Captain Murchison tells me that your boat will be as good as before after she is repaired; but if she should not be so, sell her at once for what you can get for her and order a new one, I will pay the difference. In any case I consider I owe you a boat. Whether it is five years hence or ten or fifteen, if I am alive and you want another boat I give you authority to order one of the best that can be built, and to tell them to send the bill in to me. I have not given you anything for your nephew, for I have been talking to my wife, and maybe we can serve him better in some other way."

Mrs. Godstone had indeed been in for a chat each day with Jack's mother, and had told her husband that she felt sure neither Mrs. Robson nor Jack would like an offer of money.

"The lad is very intelligent," she said, "and he and his mother are of quite a different class to the fisher people here. His father was a gentleman, and she has the manners of a lady. I should like for us to do the boy some permanent good, William."

"Well, we will see about it, my dear," her husband had said. "As soon as I am well enough to talk to him I will find out what his own wishes in the matter are."

Jack was therefore sent for after his uncle had left the inn.

"Well, my lad," Mr. Godstone said as he entered, "I am glad to see you at last and to thank you for what you did for us the other day. My wife tells me that you do not like being thanked, and as deeds are better than words we won't say much more about it. So I hear you have only been living here about two years?"

"That is all, sir; we lived at Dulwich before."

"So I hear. And your father was an artist? Have you any taste that way?"

Jack shook his head. "No, sir; I never thought of being an artist. I always wanted to go to sea."

"To go to sea—eh?" Mr. Godstone repeated. "Well, then, you have got your wish."

"Oh, I do not call this going to sea," Jack said contemptuously. "I mean, I wanted to be a sailor—not a fisherman."

"And why didn't you go then, lad?"

"Well, sir, in the first place mother did not know anyone who had to do with ships; and then her friends were all here, and she knew the place and its ways, and she thought that by buying a bawley, as she has done, in time I should come to sail her and earn my living as my uncle does. And then I don't think she would ever have agreed to my going to sea right away from her; but I do not know about that."

"Well, lad, you see the case is changed now. I have to do with ships, and Captain Murchison here commands one. At least he doesn't at the present moment, but he will do as soon as I can buy another to supply the place of the *Petrel*. And as he saw one yesterday that he thinks highly of, I shall probably buy her as soon as she has been surveyed. So you see that difficulty is at an end. As to your mother, no doubt she would have objected to your going as a ship's-boy, but perhaps she wouldn't if you were going as an apprentice. We call them midshipmen on board our ships; I like the name better than apprentice, though the thing is about the same. Captain Murchison will, I am sure, be glad to have you with him, and will do his best to make a good sailor of you. And you may be sure that I shall push you on if you deserve it as fast as possible; and it may be that in another ten years you will be in command of one of my ships. Well, what do you say to that?"

"Oh! thank you, sir," Jack exclaimed. "I should like that better than anything in the world, if mother will let me."

"I don't think that your mother will stand in the way of your good," Mr. Godstone said. "And she must see that the prospect is a far better one than any you can have here; for after all, the profits of a bawley are not large, and the life is an infinitely harder one than that of a sailor. You had better not say anything to your mother about it until my wife has had a chat with her."

CHAPTER VII.

ON BOARD THE "WILD WAVE."

MRS. GODSTONE found no difficulty whatever in persuading Jack's mother to allow him to take advantage of her husband's offer. Mrs. Robson had at her husband's death decided at once that, with the small sum of money at her disposal, the only method she could see of making ends meet was to go down to Leigh and invest it in a bawley. She had never told Jack that she had even thought of allowing him to carry out his wish to go to sea; but she had thought it over, and had only decided on making a fisherman of him after much deliberation. The desire to keep him with her had of course weighed with her, but this was a secondary consideration. She had so decided, because it was evident that had he gone to sea it must have been as a ship's-boy. In such a rough life he would have had no time whatever to continue his studies, and would speedily have forgotten most that he had learned, and he might have remained many years before the mast before he could pass as a third mate. She thought therefore that he would do better by remaining at Leigh and becoming in time master of a bawley.

In the two years that had passed she had come to have doubts as to whether she had decided wisely. The profits of fishing were exceedingly small, and the prospects were but poor. She knew well that her husband had hoped that his son would follow some line that would maintain him in his own rank of life, and she fretted at the thought that Jack would settle down for life as a Leigh fisherman, and that Lily would probably in time become a fisherman's wife. When therefore Mrs. Godstone told her that her husband was ready to place Jack on board one of his ships as midshipman, and that he would take care he had every chance of making his way up, Mrs. Robson thankfully accepted the offer.

"The boy has always wished for a life at sea," she said; "and I am thankful indeed that he should have such a chance of getting on. I am most grateful to Mr. Godstone for his offer, and most gladly accept it."

"It is the least my husband can do, Mrs. Robson, considering the share your son took in saving his life. But you must not consider that this discharges the debt that I owe for myself and Mildred. That is another matter altogether. Now, in the first place, I am sure you must wish sometimes that your little girl could have an education of a different kind to that which she can obtain here. Now, I should like to send her to a good school where she would be well educated. We need not look farther forward than that at present. She is only ten years old now, and in another seven or eight her brother may be a second mate, and, with the prospect of becoming a captain in another three or four, would like his sister to be educated as a lady."

"You are very kind, Mrs. Godstone," Mrs. Robson said with tears in her eyes. "But in the first place, I don't think I could bring myself to part with her, and in the second, I do not like to take advantage of your kindness."

"The second reason is absurd," Mrs. Godstone said decidedly. "Suppose instead of saving all our lives your son had helped to get out anchors and had got the ship off, he would have had his share of the salvage, which might have come to many hundreds of pounds; and it is nonsense because he saved lives instead of goods there should be no reward for the service. As to your first reason, I can quite enter into it; and I know that I should not have liked to be parted from Mildred. Therefore I do not propose to send her away from you, but to do it in another way. To send your girl to a really good school will not cost less than a hundred a year, and that sum I shall be very glad to pay until she is of an age to leave school.

"Now, I understand that your principal reason in coming to Leigh was that your son should in time be able to sail your boat. That reason does not exist any longer, and you might therefore be as well anywhere else as here. Your brother can look after your interests in your boat, and you will get the same share of its profits as if you were living here. I think for your son's sake as well as your daughter's, it would be pleasanter and better that you were away from here.

"Now I am going to pay a hundred a year for your girl to be educated, but it makes no difference to me how that hundred is spent, providing she gets the education. It seems to me, therefore, that it would be better if you were to move again, say to Dulwich, where no doubt you have still friends, having lived there for so long. Then you could send her as a day-boarder in a good school for some thirty or forty pounds a year. You could still keep her with you, and have a nice home for Jack whenever he comes back from sea.

"Well, think this over. It seems to me and to Mr. Godstone to be by far the best plan for all parties. And it will be much the most pleasant to us; as I should then hope to see you often, and to see for myself how your child is getting on. Do not give an answer to me now; it will be another week before my husband can be moved up to town, so there will be plenty of time for you to look at it in all lights before you decide. I know that it will be a sacrifice for you to leave Leigh where you have so many relations and friends; but I am sure this will not weigh with you as against the interest of your children."

So saying the ship-owner's wife shook hands with Mrs. Robson and at once went out. Half-way down the street she met Jack.

"It is all settled, Jack," she said, in answer to his look. "Your mother has agreed to your going."

"Has she?" Jack exclaimed in delight. "Hurrah!

Thank you so much, ma'am," and throwing his cap in the air he caught it again, and then started home at a run at the top of his speed. Bursting in at the door he was sobered instantly by seeing his mother in tears.

"My dear mother!" he exclaimed, "don't cry over it. Of course I should like to go to sea and always wanted it, still I would not think of doing it if it makes you unhappy. Although you did tell Mrs. Godstone that you consented, I will go off at once and tell them that I have changed my mind, and that on thinking it over I have concluded to stay here with you."

"No, no, Jack," his mother said, as he turned to carry his offer into effect. "It is not that at all. I am quite willing that you should go, my boy. Of course I shall miss you; but other women have to see their sons go to sea or abroad, and I shall be no worse off than they are. I am very pleased, indeed, that you should have the life you wish for open to you. There is now a far better prospect of your getting on and doing well than there was when your father consented that you should go to sea some day. I am not crying about that at all, Jack, but from pleasure, with perhaps a little pain in it, at the kind offer

Mrs. Godstone has just made me with regard to Lily and myself."

And she then told Jack the proposal that had been made to her.

"And are you going to accept it, mother? Oh, I do hope you will. I have never cared for myself, but I have sometimes been so sorry when I thought that Lily would grow up so different from what my father would have wished her."

"And so have I, Jack. Boys are boys, and can to some extent make themselves what they like. Poor men's sons can, if they are steady and industrious and clever, rise in the world; rich men's sons can come down to beggary. But it is different with girls. And it always has been a great grief to me too when I have thought of Lily's future. For myself, I do not like taking the money—that you can well believe,—but for her sake I should be very wrong to refuse the offer. I shall be sorry to leave Leigh; and yet, you see, after living for thirteen years such a different life, I do not see things as I did when I was a girl, and have blamed myself often because I have felt the difference. But I have felt it, and therefore the idea of going back to Dulwich again is not so painful to me as I think it ought to be."

"Of course it is quite natural, mother," Jack said; "and it would be curious if you did not feel so after living there so long and mixing with people so different in their ways. And won't it be splendid having a nice little home like that to come back to, and Lily being educated as a lady, and I making my way on. It will be grand, mother!"

"I shall have a talk with my father and Ben," Mrs. Robson said. "My own mind is quite made up; still I should like to speak to them before I see Mrs. Godstone again."

Tripper senior and Ben quite agreed with Mrs. Robson that she ought to accept the offer.

"We shall be always glad to see you down here, Bessy, you know, whenever you like to come; but it is certainly best for you and the young ones for you to accept the offer. It is a grand thing for Lily; and though we shall be very sorry to lose you, it would be awfully foolish to say no to such a proposal as that."

At heart, perhaps Tripper senior and his son were not altogether so very sorry that Bessy should go to London. They felt that she was now not one of themselves; and Tripper senior, who was much more fond of his glass than was good for him, felt her presence in Leigh as a sort of restraint upon himself, and had often informed Ben confidentially that Bessy had grown altogether too nice for him. When, therefore, Mrs. Godstone called again at the end of the week, Bessy thankfully accepted her offer, and it was settled that she should move up to London as soon as she could find a house. She would, she knew, have no difficulty in obtaining a tenant for her present residence; for houses were scarce at Leigh, and one so conveniently situated would find many eager for it as soon as it was generally known that it was to let.

Accordingly, two days after Mr. Godstone and his wife had left Leigh, Mrs. Robson went up to town with Jack, and going down to Dulwich had no difficulty in finding a little cottage that would suit them well, and to this a fortnight later they moved up with their belongings. The very day after they moved in, Jack received a letter from Captain Murchison telling him to come down on the following morning to St. Katharine Docks, as the *Wild Wave* had now been purchased by Mr. Godstone, and would at once be fitted out for sea.

At eight o'clock next morning Jack found himself alongside the *Wild Wave,* a fine barque-rigged ship of about eight hundred and fifty tons. A number of riggers were at work on board, and Captain Murchison was on the poop talking to an officer, whom Jack at once guessed to be the first mate.

"That's right, Jack," the captain said as the lad mounted to the poop; "nothing like getting into harness in good time. We only took possession of the barque yesterday, and have put the hands to work this morning. I thought you had better come to work at once, because there is nothing like learning things from the beginning; and if you keep your eyes open you will learn as much as to the way things should be done as you would do in six months afloat. Mr. Timmins, this is Jack Robson, who sails with us as a midshipman. He is the lad I told you of who aided in saving all our lives on board the *Petrel.* If it had not been for him and the two men with him the house of Godstone & Son would have lost its head. As the owner as well as myself owe so much to him, I am sure you will do all you can to help him to learn his work. He is not like a new hand altogether, having already had two years' experience in a fore-and-aft craft. Of course the work is very different here; still it is a capital apprenticeship, and men who can manage a bawley in such a sea as was on when the *Petrel* was wrecked are fine sailors, and would soon be at home on any craft that ever floated."

"I will do the best I can for him, Captain Murchison, and will make a sailor out of him—never fear. There is nothing for you to do on board yet, my boy, except to keep your eyes open. Watch all that is going on. This is a rigger's job; but it is well to learn how everything is done, because you may be called upon to do it any moment. Do not be afraid of asking me questions about anything you do not understand, and do not mind if I answer you sharp if I happen to be busy when you ask me—that is my way; and I daresay the riggers, when they see that you really want to learn, will be willing enough to give you a hint or two."

"I am going ashore with him now for a couple of hours, Mr. Timmins. After that he will be at your disposal."

Jack followed the captain across the gangway on to the wharf. "I am going with you to order your outfit," the captain said. "I had intended to have done it on my own account, but Mr.

Godstone would not hear of it; so I must obey orders. Your own things will do well enough until we get the riggers out of the ship and the painting done. Till then Mr. Timmins will be the only officer on board; the others will not join till she begins to take in her cargo. The second and third mates of the *Petrel* will sail with me again, and so will all the men who were rescued. Naturally they like a run ashore as long as they can; and there is nothing for them to do till the ship is out of the painter's hands."

Captain Murchison took Jack to an outfitter's in Fenchurch Street, and ordered him a complete midshipman's outfit. Then Jack went back to the docks, and for the rest of the day watched the operations of the riggers. With many of the processes he was already familiar, but he observed several differences in the methods pursued on board a large ship. As soon as he had come on board he had asked the first mate if there was any objection to his lending a hand if the riggers would allow him.

"None at all, my lad. An officer ought to be able to show his men how to do everything, and he can never do that if he is afraid of dirtying his hands. Of course you do know a good deal already about the serving and parcelling of ropes and stays, but likely enough they are done in a different fashion here to what they are on board a smack. I will speak to the head-rigger myself, and tell him you want to learn your business, and are ready to do anything that he likes to set you to; and as you have been already two years at the work he will not find you a lubber."

The rigger at once placed Jack at work with one of the gangs, and he worked steadily until four bells sounded, and the men knocked off.

"You need not get here till eight in the morning," Mr. Timmins said to him as he was about to leave. "The captain said you were living at Dulwich, and that it would take you an hour to get here; so as at present you are a sort of volunteer, it will be quite time enough if you are here by eight. I am glad to see that you are handy at your work; but that I expected. There is no better training for a sailor than a couple of years on board a smack. You learn to turn your hand to everything there very much better than you can on a large craft."

CHAPTER VIII.

ALEXANDRIA.

TEN days' hard work and the *Wild Wave's* equipment was nearly complete. The riggers were to put the finishing touch to their work that evening, and the carpenters to finish all below, and were to begin in the morning scraping and cleaning the decks, and there then remained only the painting to be done. The captain's usual hour for coming on board was eleven o'clock, but the men were just knocking off for dinner when he arrived.

"Well, Mr. Timmins, when do you think we can be ready to take cargo on board?"

"Well, sir, it will take them three days to get the decks planed. They are in a beastly state, you see. She must have had a dirty lot on board her on her last voyage, and she has picked up six months' dirt in the docks. Nothing short of planing will get them fit to be seen. Then the painters will take another four days, I should say, perhaps five, as the bulwarks and all the paint on deck must be done."

"That makes eight days' work, Mr. Timmins. I suppose we cannot set the painters at work until the carpenters are done?"

The mate shook his head. "Decidedly not, if the paint is to be worth looking at, sir. It would be throwing money and time away to begin to paint as long as the chips and dust are flying about."

"If we were to get the painting on deck done directly the carpenters knock off we might do the outside while we are taking the cargo in?"

"Yes, we might do that," the mate assented; "though even then if it is anything like a dusty cargo the paint wouldn't show up as smooth and clean as one would like to see it."

"Well, we can't help that," the captain said. "I have just come from the office, and they have had an offer for a freight, part to Alexandria and part to Smyrna; but they wanted to begin to load at once. I said that was out of the question, but that I thought I could begin to take it on board next Monday."

"Well, it will be quick work, sir. However,

if you can get them to put a good strong gang of carpenters on board they might get the deck finished off by Wednesday evening. Anyhow, we might have the painters on board on Thursday morning, and if they are sharp they should finish by the time they knock off on Saturday."

"Yes. Two coats will be sufficient," the captain said; "at any rate in most places. They might send a man or two to-morrow to put a coat at once on at the gangways and other places where it is worst."

"Do you know what the cargo is, captain?"

"Mixed cargo; some railway iron for Egypt, the rest hardware and dry goods of one sort and another, but beyond that I did not hear any particulars."

"Well, captain, I think we can say that we shall be ready to take it on board on Monday. Will you get them at the office to write to the two mates to tell them to be here the first thing in the morning?

"I think you are in luck, youngster," Mr. Timmins went on as the captain left the ship to see that a strong gang of carpenters were set to work. "A trip up the Mediterranean will be a capital breaking in for you. You will hardly be out of sight of land all the way, and Alexandria and Smyrna are two ports well worth seeing. We don't very often get a jaunt up the Mediterranean now; those rascally steamers get all the work."

When the riggers had once left the ship Jack had nothing more to do, and Mr. Timmins told him that it would be no use his coming again until Monday morning.

"You will be useful then," he said, "helping to check off the cargo as it comes on board. You had better bring your chest down and take up your quarters here. I shall get the cook in on Monday, and I expect we shall all stop on board. Of course when work is over you can always go back home when you are disposed."

To Mrs. Robson's delight, therefore, Jack was able to spend the next few days at home, and also to assure her that his first v⁓ge was to be a short one only.

All was in readiness on Monday morning. The second and third mates came on board early; the crew were not to join until the evening before sailing, as the work of loading was done by stevedores. The second and third mates were both young men. They had spoken to Jack on board the bawley, and had shaken hands with him when they left Leigh with warm expressions of gratitude, and they both greeted him most cordially as soon as they met him on the deck of the *Wild Wave*. Jack therefore commenced his career as a sailor under altogether exceptionally pleasant conditions. The captain and two of the mates were under very deep obligations to him, and Mr. Timmins had already conceived a very favourable opinion of him from his willingness to turn his hand to anything, and from his quickness and handiness.

For the next three days work went on from morning until night. Jack was stationed at one of the hatchways with the second mate checking off every box, bale, and package as it went down. The boatswain and crew came on board on the Tuesday, as there was the work of bending the sails and getting all in readiness for the start to be got through. Jack had not returned home on Monday or Tuesday night, but on Wednesday he went home to say good-bye, for the vessel was to go out of dock at noon on Thursday.

Before leaving home he donned for the first time his neat uniform, which had come only a few days before. Lily was delighted with his appearance, and his mother felt no little pride as she looked at him. and, sad as she was at the prospect of his long absence, was thoroughly convinced that the choice he had made was a wise one. Mrs. Godstone and her daughter had been down twice to call upon Mrs. Robson since her arrival at Dulwich, and on the previous Saturday Jack and his mother had gone there to dine, Captain and Mrs. Murchison being the only other guests.

After a tearful good-bye Jack started from home. On his arrival on board he found two other lads, one a year older than himself and one as much younger. Jim Tucker, the elder, had already made two or three voyages in Mr. Godstone's ships. Arthur Hill was going to sea for the first time. Jack knew that two other midshipmen were sailing in the *Wild Wave*, and found them arranging their things in the little cabin, with three bunks, allotted to them.

"Hallo! You are Robson, I suppose?" Jim Tucker began as he entered. "You have got a lot of gear here in the cabin, and you must stow it away in a smaller space than it takes up at present or we shall never fit in."

"I have not begun to stow it away yet," Jack said. "I was waiting to see how much you had both got, and which berth you were going to choose, before I began to settle at all."

"Yes, that is all right enough," Tucker answered. "Well, as I am the senior, I will take this berth under the port."

"I suppose I am next," Jack said. "I will take the top one opposite."

This being settled the lads proceeded to put things straight and stow away their portmanteaus.

As soon as they had done this they went on deck. The vessel was already warping out of the dock, and as soon as she was through the gates a steam-tug seized her and took her down the river. It was eight o'clock, and the sun was just setting, when the hawser attached to the tug was thrown off. Some of the sails had already been hoisted, for the wind was northerly. The rest were now shaken out and sheeted home, and under a cloud of white canvas—for the *Wild Wave* had been fitted with an entirely new suit of sails—the vessel proceeded on her way. The officers were divided into two watches. The first and third mates and Arthur Hill were in one watch, the second mate and the other two lads in the other.

After the constant work on board the smack Jack found it strange as he came down the river to be walking up and down the deck with nothing to do. The *Wild Wave* passed through a fleet of bawleys trawling off Hole Haven; he knew every one of them by sight, but the *Bessy* was not among them.

Meals had been irregular that day with the officers, for there was much to be seen after in coiling down ropes, washing the decks, and in getting everything neatly in ship-shape. As they passed the Middle Sunk the second mate touched Jack on the shoulder.

"That's her," he said; "at least all that remains of her," and he pointed to some black timbers just appearing above the surface of the water.

"Yes; that's her," Jack said. "I heard from my uncle that they blew her up three weeks ago."

"Rather a different scene from what it was that day," the mate, whose name was Hoare, said. "I thought it was all up with us, and even when we saw you coming we hardly believed that you could get near enough to take us off; and now it is as smooth as glass."

"It was a lucky day for me, sir, that was," Jack said. "I had then nothing to look forward to, beyond sailing a bawley; now I have got the life I always wanted to follow, and every prospect of getting on."

"That you have, my lad," Hoare agreed. "It

was a rare bit of luck for you that you made us out, no doubt, and a rare bit of luck for us too."

The voyage began well. The wind continued light and in the right quarter all the first week. Jack and his companions were not idle, and always went aloft with the watch when there was occasion to make any change with the sails. This was at first a trial for Arthur Hill; but Jim Tucker was an old hand at it, and Jack, who had often had to make his way up the *Bessy's* mast when she was rolling heavily, was soon quite at home on the yards of the *Wild Wave*. For two hours every morning the three boys worked at navigation, Mr. Hoare acting as instructor.

So smooth was the sea and so slight the motion that Jack could hardly believe that he was sailing down through the Bay of Biscay, of which he had heard so much; and he was quite surprised when, on the fifth day after sailing, Mr. Hoare pointed to land on the port bow, and told him that was Portugal.

"We have had capital luck, so far," the officer said. "If the wind does but hold till we once get fairly round Cape St. Vincent, it may change as soon as it likes into any quarter except the east, and we are not very likely to get that at this time of the year."

"I should not mind a change of wind a bit, sir," Jack said; "it would bring us something to do."

"Ah, yes; after being accustomed to go about every five minutes or so on the Thames, I understand you finding this monotonous, Jack. When you have had a little more of the sea, you won't mind how much you get of fine weather and favouring winds. As for storms, I don't care if I never see another. They are very grand to read of in books, and when you have got a stout ship and plenty of sea room there is no need to be afraid; but when you are wet through for a week at a spell, and the galley-fires can't be kept going, there is very little comfort in it."

The wind changed next day to the west, and by evening was blowing hard. A good deal of the canvas was taken off, and the ship edged further away from land; but after blowing strongly the wind abated again, and the next day the *Wild Wave* passed Cape St. Vincent and headed for the Straits of Gibraltar. As the wind still held from the west they made a rapid run, and in ten days after passing St. Vincent dropped anchor in the harbour of Alexandria.

The next day the captain said to Jim Tucker, "You three lads can go ashore after dinner to-day. There is nothing particular for you to do on board, and it is well to get a view of these foreign towns while you can. When you once get to be mates you will not have much chance to do so, for then you will have to be looking after the loading and unloading of the cargo. Come off before gun-fire. There are about as cut-throat a lot of thieves in Alexandria as in any port on the Mediterranean, and that is saying a good deal."

"It is quite possible that there will be trouble here before long," Mr. Hoare remarked at dinner.

"I saw something in the paper about it," Mr. Alston, the third mate, said; "but I did not trouble to read through the accounts. What is it all about?"

"There has been a sort of peaceable revolution," Mr. Hoare said "The colonels of the regiments in Cairo, headed by a general named Arabi Pasha, mutinied, and the viceroy had to give way to them."

"What did they mutiny about?" the third mate asked.

"Well, in the first place they wanted privileges for the army, and in the second place they wanted a lot of Europeans who hold berths to be dismissed, and the government to be entirely in the hands of natives. It is a sort of national movement, with the army at the head of it; and the viceroy, although still nominally the ruler of Egypt, is in fact little more than a cipher in the hands of Arabi and the colonels. They say the French are at the bottom of it, and it is likely enough. They have always been jealous of our influence in Egypt. However, I do not suppose we shall interfere in the matter, unless they break regularly out and ill-treat Europeans, and threaten to seize the canal or something of that sort."

After dinner the three boys landed together in a boat. Half a dozen natives pressed round them directly they stepped ashore, and offered to act as guides; but these offers they refused, for, as Jim Tucker said, "We have only got to walk about, and we are certain to find ourselves somewhere. It will be time enough talking about taking a guide when it is time for us to make down to the port again. This is a long street, let us follow it. It must lead somewhere."

Staring into the funny little shops, and at the varying crowds, composed of people of all the nationalities of the Mediterranean, mingled with a swarm of scantily-clad natives, and women wrapped up in dark blue cotton cloths, the lads made their way along.

"What an awful place for flies!" Arthur Hill said, after brushing two or three off his cheek. "Just look at that child! Why, there are a dozen round its eyes, and it doesn't seem to mind them in the least; and there is another just the same!"

"I expect the coating of dirt is so thick that they do not feel it," Jim Tucker said. "Poor little beggars, most of them look as if they had not had a wash for the last month. The women are ugly enough, what you can see of them, and that is not much. What a rascally set the Europeans look! The Egyptians are gentlemen by the side of them. I fancy from what I have heard they are the sweepings of the European ports—Greeks, Italians, Maltese, and French. When a fellow makes it too hot at home for the place to hold him, he comes over here—

"Ah! this is more like a town," he broke off as they entered the great square. "My goodness! how hot the sun does blaze down here. I say, here is a refreshment place. Sorbette—Ices. It is lucky that they put the English. Come on, you fellows, an ice would be just the thing now."

As they came out they were accosted by an Egyptian driver. "Take a carriage, gentlemen? Drive to Sweet-water Canal. See the gardens."

"What do you say, Jack?" Tucker asked. "I suppose we may as well go there as anywhere else."

"Well, we will go there later, Tucker. One does get shade in the narrow streets; but there would be no fun in driving with this sun blazing down on us. By five o'clock, when the sun gets a bit lower, it will be pleasant enough. I vote we go into the narrow streets, where we shall get shade, and see the natives in their own quarters."

The others agreed, and turning out of the square they were soon in the lanes.

"This is not half as amusing as the Indian towns," Tucker said. "Last voyage I went to Calcutta, and it is jolly in the natives' town there, seeing the natives squatting in their little shops, tinkering and tailoring, and all sorts of things. And such a crowd of them in the streets! This is a poor place in comparison, and most of the shops you see have European names over them. However, one gets the shade; that is something."

CHAPTER IX.

THE RIOT IN ALEXANDRIA.

FOR half an hour the lads sauntered on, interested in the people rather than the shops. They bought a few things. Jack invested in half a pound of Egyptian tobacco and a gaily-decorated pipe for his Uncle Ben, two little filigree brooches, and a couple of very large silk handkerchiefs of many colours, with knotted fringes, for his mother and sister.

"I do not know what they will do with them," he said; "but they will do to put on the back of a sofa or something of that sort."

The others also made some purchases, both expending a good deal more than Jack did; but the latter said that he would keep his money for Smyrna, where probably he would get all sorts of pretty things.

They were walking quietly along, when they saw a commotion in front of them. A number of men were shouting and gesticulating angrily, and blows were exchanged.

"Let us get out of this," Jack said. "It is no good running the risk of getting our heads broken."

People were now running from the shops, while from side streets the natives poured down.

"This is a regular row!" Jim Tucker exclaimed. "Look! those fellows are all armed with big sticks. Listen! there are pistols going off somewhere else."

A moment later the natives fell suddenly upon some Europeans standing close to the boys. These drew knives and pistols, and a fierce combat at once raged.

"Come out of this!" Jim exclaimed, running into a shop close by. "We must make a bolt for it somewhere."

At that moment an Italian, armed with a pistol, rushed in from behind the shop.

On seeing the three lads he exclaimed in broken English, "Shut the door, they mean to kill us all!"

The boys closed the door, and the owner piled some boxes and other goods against it; but there was no fastening up the window, for the fastenings were outside.

"Come upstairs," the man said, and the lads followed him to the floor above.

The battle was still raging in the street. Groups of Greeks and Italians stood together, defending themselves with their knives from the heavy sticks of their assailants, but were being fast beaten down. The shrieks of women rose loud above the shouting of the combatants, while from the upper windows the cracks of revolvers sounded out as the Greek, Maltese, and Italian shopkeepers who had not sallied out into the streets tried to aid their comrades below.

"Now, have you got any arms you can give us?" Tucker asked. "This looks like a regular rising of the natives. They would never all have their sticks handy if they hadn't prepared for it."

"There are some long knives in that cupboard," the man said, "and there is another pistol my brother Antonio has got. He is sick in bed."

Just at this moment the door opened and another Italian came in in trousers and shirt.

"What is it Joseph?"

"The natives have risen and are massacring all the Europeans."

The sick man made his way to the window.

"I am not surprised," he said, as he discharged his pistol and brought down a native who was in the act of battering in the head of a fallen man. "You said only yesterday, you thought there was mischief brewing—that the natives were surly and insolent; but I did not think they would dare to do this."

"Well, brother, we will sell our lives as dearly as we can."

The conflict was now pretty nearly over, and the two men withdrew from the window and closed the jalousies.

"Most of them are making off," Antonio said, peeping cautiously out through the lattice-work. "I suppose they are going to attack somewhere else. What are the police doing? They ought to be here soon."

But the time went on, and there were no signs of the police. The natives now began to break open the shops and plunder the contents. The two men placed themselves at the top of the stairs. It was not long before they heard a crashing of glass and a breaking of wood, then a number of men rushed into the shop.

"Don't fire, Joseph," Antonio said, "so long as they do not try to come up here. They may take away the soap and candles and other things if they choose, if they will but leave us alone."

The stairs were straight and narrow, and led direct from the shop itself to the floor above. After plundering the shop the natives departed laden with their spoil, without attempting to ascend the stairs.

"We are in an awful fix here," Jim Tucker said. "What do you think we had better do? Shall we get out at the back of the house and try and make a bolt of it?"

"I do not think that is any good," Jack replied. "I was at the back window just now, and could hear shouts and the report of firearms all over the place. No; if we go out into the streets we are safe to be murdered, if we stop here they may not search the house. Anyhow, at the worst we can make a better fight here than in the streets."

Two hours passed. At times large bodies of natives rushed along the streets, brandishing their sticks and shouting triumphantly. Some few of them had firearms, and these they discharged at the windows as they passed along.

"We ought to have had some troops here long before this," Antonio said to his brother.

The latter, who was sitting on a chair evidently

exhausted by his exertions, shrugged his shoulders.

"They were more likely to help the mob than to interfere with them. The troops are at the bottom of the whole trouble."

A clock on the mantel-piece struck five, just as a fresh body of natives came down the street. They were evidently bent upon pillage, as they broke up and turned into the shops. Shouts and pistol-shots were again heard.

"They are sacking the houses this time, Joseph. Now the hour has come."

The two brothers knelt together before the figure of a saint in a little niche in the wall. The boys glanced at each other, and each, following the example of the Italians, knelt down by a chair and prayed for a minute or two. As they rose to their feet there was a sudden din below. Pistol in hand the brothers rushed out on the landing.

"Do not try to come up!" Antonio shouted in Egyptian. "You are welcome to what you can find below, but you shall not come up here. We are desperate men, and well armed."

The natives, who were just about to ascend the stairs, drew back at the sight of the brothers standing pistol in hand at the top, with the three lads behind them. The stairs were only wide enough for one to advance at a time, and the natives, eager as they were for blood and plunder, shrank from making the attempt. Some of those who were farthest back began to slink out of the shop, and the others followed their example. There was a loud talking outside for some time, then several of them again entered. Some of them began to pull out the drawers, as if in the hopes of finding something that former searchers had overlooked, others passed on into an inner room.

"What are they up to now, I wonder?" Arthur Hill said.

"No good, I will be bound," Jim Tucker replied. "There! they seem to be going out again now."

Just as the last man pa.._d out Antonio exclaimed in Italian, "I smell smoke, Joseph; they have fired the house! They have set fire to the room below," he translated to the lads; but even before he spoke the boys understood what had taken place, for a light smoke poured out from the inner room, and a smell of burning wood came to their nostrils.

"The beggars have done us," Jim Tucker said bitterly. "We could have held these stairs against them for an hour, but this fire will turn us out in no time."

The smoke rose thicker and thicker, and they could hear the crackling of wood.

"Let us get out of the back window, we may get off that way."

Touching Antonio's arm he beckoned him in that direction. The Italian nodded, and the party went into the back room. Antonio drew the sheets from the beds and knotted them. Jim went to the window and looked out. As he did so there was a yell of derision from below. A score of the natives had made their way through the adjoining houses, and taken up their station from behind to cut off their retreat. It needed no words to tell those in the room what had taken place. Antonio threw down the sheets and said to his brother, "Let us sally out, Joseph; the sooner it is over the better. See, the smoke is coming up through the floor already. Let us go out before we are suffocated."

"I am ready," the other replied.

Followed by the boys the brothers left the room and descended the stairs. The flames were already rushing out of the back room. There was a shout from without as the defenders were seen to descend the ladder. The boys grasped each other's hands as a final farewell, and then with set lips and knives firmly grasped followed the two Italians and dashed into the street. Sharp cracks of the revolvers sounded out, and then in an instant the mob closed round the little party. Keeping close together, cutting and thrusting with their knives, the boys tried to make their way through. The crowd was so thick, that mixed up as they were in it, the natives could not use their sticks, but drawing their knives grappled with the boys. Jack felt a sharp pain in several places; he fell, struggled to his feet again, was again struck down. He seemed to hear a voice raised above the din, then he knew nothing more.

When he recovered his senses he found that a native was stooping over him and pressing a cloth to his forehead. He lay still for a minute or two, wondering faintly what had become of him. Looking round he could see he was in a small room. An Egyptian of the better class, in buttoned-up frock-coat and light trousers, and with a scarlet fez on his head, was standing looking down at him, and was apparently giving instructions to the native, who was endeavouring to staunch one of his wounds. As soon as he took this in, the thought of his comrades flashed across his mind, and pushing the man's hand back from his forehead he struggled into a sitting position.

"Hurrah, Jack! I was afraid that they had done for you," a voice said, and he saw Tucker and Hill sitting propped up against a wall.

Two of the natives now took hold of him, dragged him along the floor, and placed him by the side of the others. Then the Egyptian said, "You keep quiet, I save your lives. If you move or make noise we kill you at once."

The lads were all faint from loss of blood, and half stupefied from the heavy blows they had received; and after a word or two of thankfulness at finding themselves all together and alive, they lay quiet. There were two or three natives in the room, and from time to time one went out or came in with news as to what was passing in the streets. Each time there was much talk among their guards, and it was evident that they were dissatisfied with the result. The outbreak, indeed, had not been, as the boys supposed, universal; had it been, the whole European population would probably have been destroyed. It was confined to a portion only of the lower part of the town. Whether it was planned or not beforehand is a disputed point.

It began in a quarrel between some Maltese and natives; but this quarrel seemed to be accepted by the latter as a signal for a general attack, and they rushed from their houses armed with heavy sticks and knives and attacked the Europeans. Rumours had for some time been current among them that the Christians intended to conquer Egypt and to put down the Mahomedan religion, and in their excited state a spark caused an explosion. It was perhaps fortunate that it came when it did, and was confined to a comparatively small part of the town; for had it spread over the whole city the loss of life would have been great indeed, for the natives had entirely their own way from three o'clock in the afternoon until seven in the evening.

The police made no attempt whatever to put down the riot. The English and Italian consuls, immediately they heard what was going on, drove together to the governor's to call upon him to send for the troops, and to take vigorous steps to restore order. They were attacked upon the way and both wounded, but they succeeded in reaching the governor's palace. By means of the strongest representations, and by telling him that he would be held personally responsible by the Powers they represented for the consequences of the disturbance, they at last induced him to act, and at seven o'clock the troops arrived and were marched through the streets, when the natives at once dispersed to their homes.

Some seventy Europeans, including ten or twelve women, were killed, and all the shops in the quarter where the riot took place, pillaged. No damage was done in the business part of the town. There the Europeans at once armed themselves as soon as the news of the riot reached them, and formed up in the square. Strong parties were landed from the ships of war, and were prepared to give so hot a reception to the mob should they come that way, that the rioters confined their work to the quarter in which it began. The Egyptians are timid people, and the population of Alexandria were not sure that the army would go to any great length against the Europeans, or that the country in general would be with them. The outbreak was therefore rather the result of the hatred existing among the lower class against the riffraff of the various nationalities gathered in Alexandria, whose conduct frequently gave good grounds indeed for the feeling entertained against them, than of deliberate intention.

How many of the natives were killed in the fight was never known; the bodies were hastily carried away and buried by their friends as soon as the rumour spread of the arrival of the troops, and only some eight or ten of their dead were found lying in the streets. The rescue of the boys was due to the presence in the mob of a wealthy bey, who lived a short distance out of the town. This man was a brother of one of the leaders of the military insurrection at Cairo, and was in close communication with Arabi and the colonels.

He had been actively preparing for a general rising against the Europeans by the propagation of stories hostile to the latter, and by exciting the greed of the lowest classes of the town by pointing out how great was the wealth they could obtain by looting the well-filled shops and warehouses. Some of his agents had assisted to bring about the riot. But he had not intended it to go so far, and had only wished to add to the excitement and ill-feeling that prevailed, by a tumult attended with loss of life upon both sides.

He was well satisfied when he saw how eagerly the natives rushed to arms, but as soon as the conflict fairly began he had sent his men among the rioters urging them not to proceed further until the army was at hand to support them. He knew that the plunder they had obtained from the small shops would only excite their desire to appropriate the contents of the rich stores in the Europeans quarters, and was therefore well contented with what had been done. He had happened to be passing when the little party rushed from the burning house into the crowd. As they did so he caught sight of the naval uniform of the boys, and imagined that they belonged to one of the ships of war.

He saw at once that their lives might be valuable to him. If his party triumphed he could hand them over and take credit for their capture; if the great insurrection that was already planned failed, he could use them as a means of obtaining favourable terms for himself. He therefore called together two or three of his men who were in the crowd, and made his way to the scene of conflict just as the lads succumbed to their foes. With great difficulty he succeeded in rescuing them from their assailants, and then had them carried into a house hard by.

As soon as it was dark the boys were wrapped up in dark cloths and carried away through the streets. As many dead bodies were being similarly taken off by the natives no questions were asked, nor did the soldiers now scattered about interfere with their bearers. The motion started the boys' wounds into bleeding again. They had difficulty in breathing through the cloths bound round them, and when they were at last thrown heavily down upon the ground their consciousness had almost entirely left them.

CHAPTER X.

PRISONERS.

FOR two or three minutes after the door was shut and bolted not a word was spoken by the three boys. All were sorely bruised, and bleeding from many cuts and wounds, and breathless and exhausted by the way in which they had been carried along and the force with which they had been thrown down. Jack was the first to speak.

"I say, how are you both—are either of you badly hurt?"

"I don't know yet," Tucker replied. "It seems to me there is nothing left of me. I am sore and smarting all over. How are you, Arthur?"

"I don't know," Arthur said. "I wonder that I am alive at all, but I don't know that I am really much hurt."

"Well, let us try and see," Jack said.

"See!" Jim repeated scornfully. "Why, I can't see my own hand."

"Well, I mean let us find out if we can stand up and move about. We shall find out, anyhow, whether any of our bones are broken."

With some difficulty and with many exclamations of pain the lads rose to their feet.

"Are both you fellows up?" Jim asked.

"Yes.".

"Well, then, we can't be very bad, anyhow. My arms are very stiff, and it seems to me that my jacket is soaked with blood, but where it comes from I do not know. I feel as if my head and face were one mass of cuts and bruises."

"That is just how I feel, Jim," Arthur replied, and Jack agreed.

"Well, this is the rummest affair!" Jim said more cheerfully, now it seemed that none of them had sustained any very serious injury. "There were we a few hours ago eating ices and enjoying ourselves stunningly; then this frightful row took place (what it was all about I have not the least idea), and just as it seemed all up with us the fellow this place belongs to (at least I suppose it belongs to him) steps in and saves us, and then we are dragged up here and chucked into this hole."

"It seems like a dream," Arthur said.

"It is a good deal too real to be a dream, it is a mighty unpleasant reality. Well, I wish there was a little daylight so that we could see what has happened to us and tie ourselves up a bit; as it is there is nothing to do but to lie down again and try to get off to sleep. I say, won't there be a row after this, when they get to know at home what has taken place. I wonder what they are going to do with us in the morning? Do you think they mean to kill us, Jack?"

"No, I should not think there was a chance of that. This fellow would not have taken us out of the hands of the mob just for the pleasure of cutting our throats privately. Still the rough way we were carried along and thrown down here does not look as if he did it from any feeling of kindness," Jack remarked.

"No, I do not suppose he did it from kindness, Jack; anyhow, it does not look like it. Well there is no use halloing about that now, let us try and get a sleep. My head feels as if it was swollen up as big as a four-gallon keg."

Accustomed not unfrequently to get a nap when on watch under the lee of the bulwark, the hardness of the ground did not trouble the boys, and before many minutes they were all asleep.— Jack and Tucker were awakened by a shout from Arthur.

"Watch on deck!"

They started into a sitting position and looked round. A ray of sunlight was streaming in through an opening some six inches square, high up on the wall.

"Well, we are objects!" Jim said, looking at his two companions. They were indeed; their faces were bruised and stained with blood, their hair matted together. Arthur's right eye was completely closed, and there was a huge swelling from a jagged bruise over the eyebrow. Jack had received a clear cut almost across the forehead, from which the blood was still oozing. Jim's face was swollen and bruised all over, and one of his ears was cut nearly off. He was inclined to bear his injuries philosophically until Jack told him that half of his ear was gone. This put him into a furious rage, and he vowed vengeance against the whole of the Egyptian race.

"Fancy going about all one's life with half an ear. Why, every boy in the street will point at it, and one will be a regular laughing-stock. You fellows' wounds are nothing to that."

"You will have to wear your hair long, Jim; it won't be noticed much if you do."

"Don't tell me," Jim replied. "I tell you I shall be a regular sight wherever I go. I shall have fellows asking me what has happened to me. Now, had it been an arm, chaps would have been sorry for me; but who is going to pity a man for losing half an ear?"

"I don't think I would mind giving half an ear just at present for a good drink and a bucket of water to wash in."

"Nor would I," Arthur agreed.

"That is all very well," Jim grumbled. "I have lost half an ear and haven't got any water to drink."

"Well," Jack said, "I suppose they do not mean to starve us anyhow, so no doubt they will bring us something before long."

Little more was said. Their tongues were swollen, their mouths parched, they still felt dizzy and stupid from the blows they had received; so they sat down and waited. The room they were in was apparently an underground cellar, generally used as a store-room. It was about twelve feet square, and the only light was that obtained through the little opening in the wall. Jack thought as he looked at it that if one of them stood on another's shoulders he could look out and see where they were. But as that mattered nothing at present, and they were not in the mood for any exertion, he held his tongue.

In about an hour a footstep was heard descending some stairs, then bolts were undone, and two Egyptians with swords and pistols in their girdles entered. They brought with them some bread and a jar of water. Jack jumped up.

"Look here," he said, "that is all right enough to eat and drink, but we want some water to wash with. Wash, you understand?" he went on as the men looked at him evidently without comprehending. "Wash, you see,—like this;" and he went through a pantomime of washing his hands and slushing his head and face. The Egyptians grinned and nodded; they said a word to each other and then retired.

"I believe it is all right," Jack said, "and that they are going to bring some."

A long draught of water from the jar did them an immense deal of good, but none had at present any inclination to eat. Presently the steps were heard coming down the stairs again, and the men entered, bringing in a large pan made of red earthenware, and containing three or four gallons of water.

"Good men!" Jim exclaimed enthusiastically; "I will spare your lives for this when I slay the rest of your countrymen," and he shook the Egyptians warmly by the hand. "I have nothing to give you," he went on, "for they turned our pockets inside out; but I owe you one, and will pay you if I ever get a chance. Now, lads, this is glorious!"

For half an hour the three boys knelt round the pan, bathing their faces and heads. Then they stripped to the waist, and after a general wash tore strips off their shirts and bandaged the various cuts they had received on the head, shoulders, and arms. In no case were these serious, although they were deep enough to be painful.

"It's nothing short of a miracle," Jack said, "that we have got off so easily. If the beggars had not been in such a hurry to get at us that they got into each other's way they would have done for us to a certainty; but they were all slashing away together, and not one could get a fair drive at us. Well, I feel about five hundred per cent better now. Let us get on our things again and have breakfast. I feel as if I could tuck into that bread now."

Just as they had got on their clothes the door again opened, and a gigantic negro entered. He carried with him a wooden box of the shape of a bandbox. He opened this and took out a melon and three large bunches of grapes, laid them down on the ground without a word, nodded, and went out again.

"My eye, this is first-rate," Jim said in delight. "Well, you see, it is not going to be so bad after all. That chap who brought us up here is evidently friendly, though why he should have sent us the fruit by itself instead of with the bread and water I do not know. However, never mind that now; let us set to."

The boys enjoyed their breakfast immensely. They first ate the grapes; when these were finished they looked longingly at the melon, which was a very large one.

"How on earth are we to tackle that?" Jim asked. "Our knives have gone with our other things."

"Perhaps we can find something to cut it up," Jack said, getting up and turning over the litter on the floor with his foot. For two or three minutes he searched about. "Hurrah!" he exclaimed at last, " here is a bit of old hoop-iron that will do first-rate. It is not stiff enough to cut with, but I think we can saw with it, if one takes hold of each end."

Without much difficulty the melon was cut into three parts, and devoured to the rind. Breakfast over they had time to consider their situation again.

"I expect," Jack said, "this pasha or whatever he is who has got us here is waiting to see how things go. If the Egyptians get the best of it he will hand us over to Arabi, or whoever comes to be their chief. If we get the best of it he will give us up, and say that he has saved our lives. That would account, you see, for this breakfast business. He only sent us bread and water by his Egyptian fellows, and he sent us the fruit privately by that black slave of his, whom he can rely upon to hold his tongue."

"I should not be surprised if that was it, Jack. That makes it look hopeful for us, for there is no doubt in the world who will get the best of it in the end. We may not thrash the beggars for a time. Alexandria is a big place, and there are a lot of troops here, and they can bring any number more down from Cairo by rail. The crews of the ships of war here are nothing like strong enough to land and do the whole business at once; besides, they have no end of forts and batteries. I expect it will be some time before they can bring ships and troops from England to capture this place."

"But there are the Italians and French," Arthur said. "They are just as much interested in the matter as we are, for I expect there were a good many more Italians and French killed yesterday than there were English."

"Ten to one, I should think," Jim agreed. "I don't think there are many English here, except the big merchants and bankers and that sort of thing, while all the small shops seem to have either French, Italian, or Greek names over the door. Well, if it is going on like this, we can afford to wait for a bit."

"Look here, Arthur," Jack said, "I will stand under that opening, and you get on my shoulders and look out. I don't suppose you will see much, but one likes to know where one is and which way one is looking. We know we are somewhere on the high ground beside the town. We must be looking somewhere north-east by the way that gleam of sunlight comes in. Very likely you can get a glimpse of the sea." Jack placed himself against the wall, and Jim helped Arthur on to his shoulders.

"Yes, I can see the sea," Arthur said as soon as his head reached the level of the loop-hole. "I can see the outer harbour, and several ships lying there and boats rowing about."

"Well, that is something anyhow," Jim said as Arthur leapt down again. "We shall be able to see any men-of-war that come in, and form some idea as to what is going on. How thick was the wall?" Jim went on.

"I should say quite a couple of feet thick. I could only see a small patch of the water through it."

"Then I am afraid there is no chance of our working our way out," Jim said. "The only way of escape I can see would be to spring on those two fellows who bring our food. We are stronger than they are, I am sure, and we might master them."

"I don't expect we could do it without noise," Jack said. "Besides, they have got pistols, and we certainly could not master them without their being able to shout. We might manage one easy enough, if one sprang on him and held his arms and prevented him getting his pistol, and another clapped his hands over his mouth; but the three of us could not manage two silently. Besides, I should not like to hurt them after their bringing us that water to wash in."

"No; we certainly couldn't do that," the other boys agreed.

"Besides," Jack went on, "we do not know where this staircase leads. But no doubt it goes up into the house, and when we got to the top someone would see us at once; and even if we broke through there would be such a chase we should never get away, and anyhow could not pass through the town down to the port and steal a boat. No, Jim, I don't think it is the least use in the world trying to escape that way. If we could dig through the wall and make our way out at night, and get quietly down among the sand-hills by the shore, we might manage to get hold of a boat and row out to the ships; but I do not see that there is any chance of our being able to do that when we haven't got as much as a knife among us."

Jim examined the walls. "There would not be much difficulty in working through them if we had a couple of good knives, they are made of sun-dried bricks. However, we will hunt about among this rubbish and see if we can find some more bits of iron. Anyhow, we can wait a day or two before we make up our minds about it and see what comes of it. I vote we clear up this litter a bit, and chuck it out through the opening. There is a close, musty smell in the place. The opening will be very handy for chucking everything out and keeping the place as clean as we can."

"Yes, Jim; but the rubbish will be very useful to us if we decide to try to cut our way out, as we can put a lot of brick-dust and stuff under it. It would not do to throw that out of the window, for it would be seen at once by anyone passing."

"Yes; you are right there, Jack. Well then, we have nothing to do but to take it as easy as we can."

The closest search through the rubbish did not bring to light any other piece of iron, and the bit they had used as a knife was so thin and rusted as to be altogether useless for the purpose for which they required it.

The days passed slowly. The two Egyptians brought bread and water regularly, and the Nubian as regularly additions to their meal—sometimes fruit, sometimes a dish of meat. Three bundles of maize straw were brought down the first evening to serve as beds for them, and on the following morning three or four men came down and swept up all the rubbish from the floor. Once every two days they were taken out under a guard of three men with swords and muskets, and allowed to sit down in the sun, with their backs against the wall, for an hour or two. The shipping still lay in the harbour, over which they commanded a good view; and after a few days they saw that several more vessels of war had entered it.

"I can see that the boats are going backwards and forwards to the shore," Jim said, "so there is no regular war begun yet."

"Look, Jim, over there to the right," Jack said. "There is a swarm of men at work. I believe they must be getting up a fresh battery there. That looks as if the Egyptians had made up their minds to fight."

"So much the worse, Jack. I don't mind how much they fight when we are out of their hands (we know what will come of that when it begins), but if they fight while we are here it may turn out bad for us, whichever way it goes."

CHAPTER XI.

THE BOMBARDMENT.

WHILE the riot had been going on, a considerable proportion of the European community of Alexandria had taken refuge on board the ships in the harbour, the men who remained behind to protect their property sending off their wives and children. Many returned on shore as soon as it was known that the troops had arrived, but the alarm was by no means abated when it was seen next day by the manner of the soldiers that they sympathized entirely with the rioters. In two or three days a large proportion of the garrison of Cairo arrived, and Arabi himself came to Alexandria. No steps were taken to punish those concerned in the riot, although many were known to the Europeans who had escaped.

The khedive was evidently powerless. The remonstrances of the European consuls were received by Arabi's council with contempt, and it was too evident to all that the riot had been but the beginning of a very much more serious affair. The women and children remained on board the ships; but the Europeans reopened their shops and continued business as usual, encouraged by the fact that not a day passed without vessels of war of one European power or another arriving in port. These had been despatched in all haste upon the news being received of the riot in Alexandria, and of the threatening aspect of affairs there.

In ten days after the outbreak there were in port English, French, Italian, Spanish, and German ships of war, and the European community now regained confidence, believing that with so powerful a fleet close at hand the Egyptians would not venture upon any fresh act of aggression.

Captain Murchison had been engaged in business connected with the cargo at the office of one of the principal merchants, when one of the clerks ran in with the news that there was a serious riot in the native part of the town, and it was said that the Europeans had been massacred. The office was at once closed, and the strong shutters put up. The clerks and employés were armed and placed in readiness to defend the place against an attack, and then Mr. Spratt and Captain Murchison went out to the great square to see what was going on. The greatest confusion reigned there. Numbers of women and children, the families of the Italian and Greek shop'keepers, were hurrying past on their way down to the port.

The shops and offices had been hastily closed and barricaded. The clerks of the great mercantile houses and banks were turning out rifle in hand. The wildest rumours prevailed as to the extent of the riot, and it was not until two hours after the commencement of the disturbance that the consuls, finding that they could obtain no aid from the governor, took upon themselves to summon aid from the two ships of war that happened to be lying in the port. The appearance of two hundred sailors fully armed and ready for action at once restored confidence among the Europeans, and prevented the riot from extending.

Upon his return to his ship after the arrival of the Egyptian troops and the termination of the riot, Captain Murchison was astonished and alarmed to hear that the three boys had not returned. He at once went on shore again, and remained for some hours making inquiries for them, but without obtaining any information whatever. The next morning he renewed the search. Matters had now settled down a little, and the shops were reopened. Going to the various restaurants in the great square he learned that three young officers had come in and eaten ices at one of them between two and three o'clock the day before, but he could learn nothing further.

He went to the English consul. The latter sent a dragoman with him to the head of the police, who promised to have inquiries made. The first and second mates also went on shore and joined in the search. They agreed the best way would be that they should take various streets leading from the square and inquire at every European shop if three lads in European uniform had been noticed. For some time no success attended them; but at last they met with a Maltese at whose shop Jack had purchased two little filigree brooches. He said he had noticed that after they left his shop they walked down the street which led directly to the spot where the riot had began, and where the greater proportion of Europeans had lost their lives. The two officers went down to the scene of the riot, but could obtain no further information respecting the missing lads.

The Europeans who had remained shut up in their houses while the riot was going on had all left immediately order was restored. The whole of the shops were wrecked and plundered, two or three houses had been burned down, and dark stains in the roadway showed where men had fallen and died.

"I fear there is no doubt whatever," Captain Murchison said, when the two mates reported to him the result of their inquiries, "that the lads must have been just at the spot where the riot broke out; the time at which they passed exactly answered to it. But in that case what could have become of them? Mr. Cookson has shown me the official list of the killed as far as it is known at present. Their bodies have all been found; but neither in that list, nor in the list of the wounded, is there any mention of three young English lads. If they had been killed their bodies would have been found with the others, and indeed their uniforms would have at once attracted attention."

"What in the world can have become of them? Could they have been in one of the houses that is burned?" Mr. Hoare suggested.

"I should hardly think that possible," the captain said. "Their remains would have been found, and would have been returned in the list as three persons unrecognized; but all the bodies seem to have been identified."

"Perhaps they have been carried off, and are prisoners somewhere," Mr. Timmins suggested.

"That is more likely, Mr. Timmins. They may have been taken for midshipmen belonging to one of the ships of war, and have been seized by someone in the hope of getting a handsome ransom for them. Anyhow, I cannot believe that they are dead; or, at any rate, if they have been killed, it has not been in a fight in the street, or their bodies must have been found. I am most anxious about them, but I cannot believe that the worst has happened to them."

Captain Murchison had bills printed in English, French, Italian, and Egyptian and distributed through the town, offering a reward for any information that would lead to the discovery, either dead or alive, of the missing lads. The bills met with no response. The Egyptians engaged in the attack upon the shops, who alone could have furnished information regarding the boys, were afraid to come forward, as they could not have done so without admitting their share in the massacre. As he could do nothing more, Captain

Murchison left the matter in the hands of Mr. Cookson, the English consul, and a week after the riot the *Wild Wave* sailed for Smyrna, Captain Murchison saying that he should look in at Alexandria on his way back, and that the boys if found were to await his return there. He did not write home to announce their disappearance; his belief that they must be still alive was strong, and he was unwilling to plunge their friends into anxiety and grief until a further time had been allowed to elapse.

For a long time negotiations went on between Admiral Seymour, who commanded the British fleet now at the port of Alexandria, and the government of the khedive. The ministers were really nothing more than the nominees of Arabi and the army, and the demands of the English admiral for satisfaction for the outrages, compensation to the sufferers, and the punishment of the guilty, were met with evasive answers. So threatening and insolent was the bearing of the Egyptian troops, that the greater part of the European population again left their houses and took refuge on board the ships in the harbour.

More and more peremptory became the demands of the English admiral, but still no results were obtained. Egyptian troops now commenced throwing up fortifications at points commanding the position of the British ships in the harbour. The admiral sent ashore and insisted that these works should be at once discontinued. No attention was paid to the demand. A message was then sent through the consuls warning all Europeans in the town to embark at once, and an ultimatum was despatched to the Egyptian ministry, saying that unless the works were stopped and a satisfactory answer to the demands returned before nightfall the ships would open fire the next day; in the afternoon, as no reply had been received, the men-of-war steamed out of the harbour and took up their position off the town.

The warships of the other nationalities also left the harbour; but as their governments refused to support actively the action of the English, they either steamed away or anchored at a distance as spectators of the approaching event. The various merchant-ships in harbour also sailed out, all of them crowded with fugitives from the town. The English fleet consisted of the *Invincible, Monarch, Penelope, Sultan, Alexandria, Superb, Inflexible,* and *Temeraire,* with the gun-boats *Signet, Condor, Bittern, Beacon,* and *Decoy.*

THE EVE OF THE CONFLICT. 161

Nearly a month had passed since the lads had been taken prisoners. They were in absolute ignorance as to what was going on in the town, except that they had been told by one of their guards, who spoke a few words of English, that Arabi and his troops were masters of Alexandria, and that every European in Egypt would be destroyed.

"They may be masters of Alexandria at present," Jim Tucker said to his comrades as they talked the matter over, "but they won't be masters long. It is possible enough that they may cut the throats of all the Europeans in Egypt, but they will have to pay dearly for it if they do. I do not believe they will keep Alexandria long. Just look at all those men-of-war in the harbour. Why, there are white ensigns flying over a dozen of them! I suppose they are wasting time palavering at present, but when the time for action comes you see they will astonish these Egyptians."

"That fellow said this morning that there were twenty thousand troops in the town," Jack said.

"If there were a hundred thousand it would make no odds, Jack."

"It would make no odds about our blowing the place up, Jim, but it would make a lot of odds if it came to landing. I do not suppose they could land more than a couple of thousand sailors from the fleet, if they did as much, and though I have no doubt they could lick about five times their own number in the field, it would be an awkward business if they had to fight their way through the narrow streets of the town."

"Well, I suppose there will be some ships along with troops soon," Jim said. "It would take them a fortnight or three weeks to get ready, and another fortnight to get out here. Perhaps they waited a week or so to see whether the Egyptians were going to cave in before they began to get ready; but at any rate there ought to be troops here in another fortnight."

The next morning early four of their guards came down and motioned them to follow them. They were evidently in high glee. Among them was the one who spoke English.

"Come along, you English boys," he said. "Big fight going to begin. You see the forts sink all you ships in no time."

"Well, we shall see about that," Tucker muttered as they followed their guard. "Perhaps you are crowing too early, my fine fellow."

"At any rate," Arthur Hill said, "we may thank them for giving us a view of it."

The guards led them to a spot where six or seven other men, all like themselves armed with muskets, were standing or sitting on a bank which commanded a view of the port and the sea beyond it. The boys threw themselves on the ground and looked at the panorama stretched away before them. They could see the two great ports, known as the Old and New Ports, with the peninsula jutting out between them, on which stood the khedive's palace, named Ras-el-tin, and other important buildings. Beyond stretched a long spit of land parallel with the shore, and sheltering the two ports.

This spit was studded with forts, which formed the principal defences of Alexandria, although there were several forts, among them Forts Mex and Marabout, on the mainland near the mouths of the harbour. Most of these forts had been erected under the superintendence of French engineers, and were considered capable of defending the town against any naval force that could be brought against it. They were armed with heavy artillery of the best modern construction.

The ports were entirely clear of shipping, but ranged along facing the forts lay the eight British ironclads. Four of them faced the forts at Ras-el-tin and the mouth of the harbour, three lay off the Mex Batteries, and one off a fort commanding what was known as the Boghaz Channel, while the little group of gun-boats lay out beyond the line of battle-ships.

Further away to the east could be seen a great number of sailing-boats and steamers. Just at seven o'clock a great puff of white smoke broke out from the black side of the *Invincible*, which was carrying the admiral's flag, and even before the sound reached the ears of the little party on the hill similar bursts of smoke spurted out from the other vessels. Then came the deep roar of heavy artillery, mingled with the rushing sound of their huge missiles through the air. Almost immediately an answering fire broke out from all the batteries fringing the sea.

In a minute or two the hulls and lower masts of the men-of-war were entirely hidden in clouds of white smoke. The very ground seemed to shake with the thunder of the heavy guns, mingled with which came the sharper sound of some of the smaller artillery in the forts and the long rattle of the machine-guns in the tops of the men-of-war. So terrible was the din that the Egyptians ceased their chatter and sat in awed silence. The shell from the Egyptian guns could be seen bursting over the vessels, while jets of water spurting out far to seaward in all directions marked the course of the round shot.

"It is downright awful, isn't it?" Arthur Hill said in a hushed voice. "I've often thought I should like to see a sea-fight, but I never thought it would be as terrible as this."

"No more did I, Arthur," Jack agreed. "I feel just as I have done when I have been out in the bawley and a big thunder-storm has burst overhead. If it feels like this here, what must it be on board a ship?"

"I don't believe it is half so bad there," Jim Tucker said. "They are all hard at work there at those big guns, and haven't got much time to think about it. I wish we could see what harm the shot are doing them. They have got some tremendous guns in some of the forts—pretty well as big as they are on board."

For an hour there was no change whatever in

the state of things, then the little gun-boats were seen to be in motion. Steaming away to the west, they engaged the Marabout Fort, which had hitherto taken its part in the fray without any return on the part of the assailants.

"I believe the fire of the forts is slackening," Jack said. "Look at that fort at the entrance to the harbour, its outline is all ragged and uneven. I wish the wind would freshen up a bit, to let us see a little more of what is going on."

Another hour and it was evident to them all that the fire of the forts was nothing like as heavy as it had been at first, while the guns of the fleet continued to thunder as steadily as when they first commenced. At twelve o'clock several of the forts had ceased to fire altogether. At one, the gun-boats having silenced the Marabout Fort, joined the three men-of-war in the bombardment of the Mex Batteries, and the *Temeraire*, having silenced the fort at the entrance of the Boghaz Channel, joined in the attack on the Ras-el-tin and Pharos Forts.

At three o'clock there was a tremendous explosion in the Pharos Fort, and now only an occasional gun answered the fire of the assailants. This soon ceased, and at four some signal flags were seen to run up to the masthead of the *Invincible*, and instantly the fire from the British ships ceased, and a dead silence succeeded the din of battle that had continued almost unbroken for nine hours.

CHAPTER XII.

FREE.

FOR two or three hours before the cessation of bombardment flames had been bursting out from several buildings in the neighbourhood of the palace of Ras-el-tin. These being in the line of fire, had doubtless been struck by shell from the ships passing over the forts in front.

When the fire ceased the Egyptians rose and motioned the boys to return to their prison.

"Well, you see, my friend," Jack said to the man who spoke English, "you have not sunk the English vessels in a few minutes, as you talked about. Not even one of the little gun-boats; and as far as I can see from here you have not even damaged them."

The man made no reply. To him and his comrades the escape of the British ships was a mystery. That they were made of iron they understood, but had no idea of the enormous thickness of their sides; and could not even imagine that ships could be built sufficiently strong to keep out the missiles discharged by the immense cannons in the forts. That not even a mast should have been knocked away seemed to them almost miraculous. In point of fact the ships had been struck but once or twice with the shells from these massive cannon. The Egyptian gunners were unaccustomed to the use of the huge pieces, and had consequently aimed too high, and the shell had passed either between the masts or far overhead.

Upon the other hand the smaller guns had been worked with accuracy, but their missiles had dropped harmless from the iron plates of the ships. The fire of the men-of-war had, in the first place, been directed mainly against these great cannon. The machine-guns in the top had created terrible havoc among the men who were carrying on the laborious and to them difficult operation of loading them, while the huge shell from the great guns had carried wholsesale destruction among them. Thus the powerful guns upon which the Egyptians had relied to beat off any attack from the sea had been fired but seldom, and one by one had been dismounted or rendered unserviceable by the fire from the ships.

The gallantry with which the Egyptian gunners stuck to their work was the object of surprise and admiration to the British sailors. It seemed scarce possible that men could work under so tremendous a fire as that to which they were exposed. The forts were literally torn to pieces, and at the end of the day were little better than heaps of ruins scattered thickly with the corpses of the Egyptian artillerymen.

"Well, what do you suppose they will be up to next, Jim?" Arthur Hill asked when the door had again closed upon them.

"I suppose they will begin again to-morrow if these fellows have not had enough of it. You see, they hardly fired a gun for the last three hours, and as far as we could see the forts were pretty well knocked to pieces; the one at the mouth of the harbour blew up, and there were several other explosions. They held out a lot better than I thought they would do, I must say, but I cannot believe they will be fools enough to go on to-morrow."

They chatted for some time as to the chances of surrender or of resistance to the last, and as to what was likely to befall themselves; then, wearied with the excitement of the day their voices became more and more drowsy and they dosed off upon their heaps of straw. Jack was the first to wake. He sat up and looked round, puzzled for a time.

"I say, wake up you fellows!" he exclaimed suddenly. "There is a tremendous fire somewhere."

The others sat up at once. They had been asleep for some hours and night had fallen, but there was a red glow of light in the cell.

"Here, Arthur, you jump up on my shoulders," Jim said, standing under the opening in the wall.

Arthur climbed up, and uttered an exclamation as his eyes became level with the opening. "I cannot see the town, but I think it must be all on fire; it is almost as light as day outside, the whole air is full of sparks and red clouds of smoke. It is tremendous!"

"Jump down and let us have a look," Jim said impatiently, and he and Jack had by turns a view of the scene. A quarter of an hour later the door opened suddenly and four of their guards ran in.

"Come, quick!" one of them said, and seizing the boys by their wrists they hurried them up the stairs. The house was in confusion. Men were packing up bundles and the bey giving directions in an angry voice. As soon as his eye fell on the boys he gave an order in Egyptian.

"Take off your clothes, quick!" The guard translated the order.

It was evidently no time for hesitation. The boys took off their waistcoats, jackets, and trousers, then the guard picked up from a bundle lying beside him three women's dresses, and wound them round them, bringing an end as usual over the head and falling down to the eyes. Then he put on the thick blue veil, extending across the face just under the eyes and falling down to the waist. The disguise was thus completed, and the three boys were transformed into Egyptian peasant women, of whom only the eyes were visible.

Another five minutes all were ready, and the bey with ten or twelve men and the boys started out from the house. Most of the men carried muskets, all had large bundles upon their shoulders. As they issued from the house the boys obtained a full sight of the city, and uttered a simultaneous exclamation as they did so. Half the city appeared to be in flames. A sea of fire extended from the port over the European quarter, including the great square, while in many other parts separate conflagrations were raging.

There was, however, no time to pause to examine the scene. The party hurried along until they came down upon the road leading across the narrow strip of land running between the two inland lakes. It was crowded with fugitives: mixed up pell-mell together were Egyptian soldiers in great numbers, and the population of the town—men, women, and children. For four hours they walked along. Then the throng along the road thinned; the Egyptian drums were sounding, and the soldiers turned off and lay down in the fields, ready to form into regiments again in the morning.

The rest of the fugitives, feeling that they were now beyond danger of pursuit, soon followed their example. The party to which the boys belonged kept on for a short distance further and then turned off. They followed a by-road for a quarter of a mile, and then stopped at a farm building. On their knocking at the door a peasant came out, but at a word from the bey he at once drew aside for the party to enter. The bey took possession of the cottage, and the men leaving their bundles inside threw themselves down on the ground without and were soon fast asleep. The idea that their captives might escape did not even occur to them.

The boys had thrown themselves down a little apart from the rest.

"This is a nice go," Jim said. "I suppose this chap is taking us off as hostages, and we may be dragged about like this for any time; for until an army is got together and conquers the whole country, I do not see how we are going to be released."

"I don't see what there is to prevent us going straight back again," Jack said; "we have got splendid disguises and might go anywhere."

"That is not a bad idea, Jack; but how are we to do it? Every one is coming the other way."

"Yes, I don't think we can go back by that road," Jack agreed; "but we might get round the other side of the lake, I should think."

"But how are we to do that, Jack? We do not know anything about the country."

"No, we do not know much about it, Jim; but I remember the day before we landed, when we were looking at that book Mr. Hoare lent us so as to get up something about Alexandria before we landed, there was a map of the town. I remember that the lake behind it, called Mareotis or some such name, extended some eight or ten miles to the west of the town, and is only separated from the sea by the high beach on which the Mex Forts stand. I do not see why we should not work round there, and get down on to the beach and make our way on to the town. Our fellows are sure to land to-morrow morning and take possession of it. We have passed across the isthmus between the two lakes, so the one we want to get round must lie somewhere to the north-west. Anyhow, the fire will be a guide to us. If we keep rather to the left of that we must strike the lake, and have only got to follow that to keep right."

"I am with you," Jim said. "What do you say, Arthur?"

"I am game," Arthur replied, "but let us be off at once. What time do you think it is?"

"I have no idea. I don't know how long we slept, but it was quite dark except for the fire, so it must certainly have been past eight o'clock. We set out half an hour later. I should say that it must be between twelve and one now, if not later. It will begin to get light again soon after four, so we have no time to lose."

"Well, let us crawl away as quietly as we can," Jack said. "I think those chaps are all asleep, but we cannot be too careful until we get a bit away from them."

The boys found it very difficult to crawl in their female garments, but kept on as noiselessly as possible until some distance from the cottage, then they stood up. They followed the lane until they came to the road, crossed the line of railway beyond it and swam the fresh-water canal, and then, guided by the glare of light over Alexandria, made their way across the fields. After half an hour's walking they found themselves on the shore of the lake. It was low and swampy, and they had to keep some distance from its edge. The reflection of the light on its smooth surface enabled them to follow its direction as well as if they had been walking close to it. They kept on until morning broke, by which time the glare of light above Alexandria lay due north of them.

"We had better lie up here," Jim said. "There is sure to be a village near the lake, and the first person who came across us and questioned us would find us out."

"I shall not be sorry to stop at all," Jack said, "for these loose yellow slipper things are horrid for walking in. I have tried going barefoot for a bit, but there are prickly things in the grass and I soon had to give that up."

There was no difficulty in finding shelter, for in many places belts of high rushes bordered the lake. Entering one of these for some little distance, and pressing down a lot of the rushes to make a dry bed on the damp earth, the lads lay down and were soon fast asleep. The sun was blazing high overhead when they awoke.

"My eye, isn't it hot!" was Jim Tucker's first exclamation. "It is enough to roast a fellow alive."

"It is hot," Jack agreed; "and the worst of it is there isn't anything to eat."

"No, and there is not likely to be," Jack replied, "till we get to Alexandria. There are the guns of the fleet still at it. It is evident that the forts have not surrendered. I don't see how we can possibly get along past those forts on the beach to the west as long as they hold out, besides it is not likely that there has been a landing from the ships yet, and the rabble of Alexandria will be plundering and killing We shall be safer anywhere than there."

"So we should," Jack agreed. "But there is one

thing quite certain, we cannot stop here without food or water. We might perhaps do without grub for a day or two, but certainly not without water. There is maize and grain ripe in the fields, so we shall do well enough for eating."

"I suppose they must have wells. People must drink here, Jack."

"I suppose there must be wells," Jack said doubtfully. "But, you see, the water in this lake is salt, and I should say they get no fresh water anywhere near, because the ground is so sandy. I rather expect they get it in small channels from the fresh-water canal."

"Well, anyhow, we can get water there," Arthur Hill said. "I vote we go back there again. Not of course anywhere near where the Egyptians are; though I do not know whether that would make much difference, for we should be on one side of the canal and they on the other. Still, we had better go beyond them; then we can, as you say, keep ourselves going by picking maize or corn or whatever we can find for a day or two, till we hear the firing cease."

There are sure to be some boats somewhere on this lake," Jack said, "and we might get hold of one and go across to Alexandria some night, and reconnoitre. If we find there are no sailors or troops there, we can take to our boat and pull back again. I think it would be better to do that than to try to work round by the sea-shore, for I believe they have fortifications running across from the sea to the lake, so as to prevent the place from being attacked by a force landing beyond the forts."

"Well, I vote we set out at once," Jim Tucker said. "I am frightfully thirsty. There are very few houses as far as I can see; if we keep a sharp look-out we ought to be able to manage so as not to meet anyone. If any peasant does run against us and asks questions, so much the worse for him."

The others agreed, and they at once started across the country, which was only cultivated here and there. They laid their course so as to strike the canal at a point some miles higher up than that at which they had left it. They only saw a few peasants in the fields, and made detours so as not to come near any of these. On the way they picked a dozen heads of maize, but were too thirsty to attempt to eat them. After three hours walking the vegetation became brighter and greener, the cultivated fields thicker, and in another half hour they stood on the bank of the canal. They went down to the edge, knelt down and took a long drink.

"Shouldn't I like a dip!" Arthur Hill said.

"We will have one, Arthur, when it gets dark; it would never do to bathe now. I do not see a soul about, but still someone might come up on the further bank at any moment, and our white skins would betray us at once. Now we have had a good drink we can hold on. We will go back again now, and sit down among the bushes and eat our corn."

When they had finished their meal the boys agreed that maize eaten raw was not by any means desirable food; however, it satisfied their hunger, and they sat discussing their plans until evening. They agreed that Arthur Hill's plan was certainly the best.

"We will give them one more day," Jim Tucker said. "I vote we stop here to-night, then have a good drink in the morning and then start back again, keeping along the canal here until we are close to the lake; then we will have another good drink and start out and walk along the lake until we find a boat, then we will hide away somewhere near it and cross after it gets dark."

It was agreed that this plan should be carried

out, and after a good night's rest they started again next morning. They kept down by the foot of the bank of the canal, and followed it until they saw the lake stretching away on the left, then they went up and had another drink.

"Hurrah!" Arthur Hill exclaimed, as he picked up a broken earthenware pot, which had apparently been thrown out by some passing boat; "this will hold a quart of water. That will give us a drink each to-night."

As they walked they had heard the heavy guns still booming over the sea, and was by no means certain that the troops had yet landed. However, they determined not to put off their expedition across the lake if they could find a boat. Carrying their jar of water carefully with them, they struck across to the lake and followed it as before, keeping a careful look-out for boats. They had proceeded about two miles along its edge, when they saw the stern of a boat projecting beyond the rushes that fringed the water's edge, and pushing more rapidly forward they came upon a beaten path through the reeds, and following this came upon a low flat boat, very roughly constructed.

"It is not much of a craft," Jim Tucker said; "but it will do for us capitally. Now, we have only to lie down and take things quietly until dark. I fancy it is about three o'clock in the afternoon now by the sun."

They lay down among a clump of bushes a short distance from the lake, and as soon as the sun had set went back to the boat again. They had already made another meal, and had finished their maize and water. They stood by the boat waiting until it should become perfectly dark, and looking across the tranquil sheet of water at the distant town, over which the smoke still hung heavily, and as the sky darkened flashes of fire could be seen. They were at last just going to get on board when they heard an exclamation of surprise behind them. Looking round they saw two natives, who had evidently come down with the intention of going out in their boat.

CHAPTER XIII.

AMONG FRIENDS.

THE astonishment of the two natives at seeing, as they supposed, three women standing with their boat, was no less than that of the boys at being thus suddenly surprised. Suspecting no harm, however, they at once moved forward, asking in Egyptian, "What are you doing here with our boat?"

"Down with them, boys!" Jim Tucker exclaimed, and at once threw himself upon one of the boatmen, while Jack and Arthur instantly sprang upon the other.

Wholly unprepared for the attack, the men were thrown down almost without resistance.

"Get some rope from the boat, Arthur!" Jim Tucker exclaimed.

Leaving Jack to hold the prostrate man, Arthur Hill jumped on board the boat, and in a minute returned with two pieces of rope. With these the arms and legs of the natives were soon firmly tied.

"Now, what are we going to do next?" Jim Tucker asked.

"It would not do to leave them here," Jack said. "If they managed to untie each other they would give the alarm, and if we had to come back we should be caught. If they could not manage to untie each other they might lie here and die. I think we had better take them with us."

"I suppose that will be the best plan," Jim agreed. "I do not know that it will make much difference in the end, for they must be left tied somewhere; still, it would certainly make it safer for us."

Accordingly the men were lifted into the boat and laid down in the bottom. Then the boys threw off the female garments, and taking the long poles punted the boat out into the lake. The water was so shallow, that it was not until they had gone more than a mile from shore that they laid in the poles and took to the clumsy oars. An hour's rowing, and the shore began to rise high in front of them. As they approached it they stopped rowing, and listened attentively.

"Now, before we go any nearer we had better gag these fellows," Jack said. "If they were to set-to to shout as soon as we had landed, our chance of getting back again would be at an end."

They tore off two strips from the cloths, rolled them up, and put them in the prisoners' mouths, putting some lashings across so that they could not get them out; then they put the men so far apart in the boat that they could not touch each other, and lashed them in these positions. This done they again wrapped themselves in their women's garments, and quietly rowed to the shore. They had but little fear of finding anyone here. The natives, if no landing had been effected from the ships, would be all engaged in the work of plundering; while if the English had taken possession of the town they would probably be keeping in their houses. No one was near when they landed, and fastening the head-rope of the boat to a stone they pushed her gently off again.

"If anyone should come along," Jim said, "it is too dark for them to see those fellows lying in the boat. Now, we must take our bearings accurately as we go along, so as to be able to find the boat again if things go wrong with us."

They had landed half a mile beyond the town, and now made their way towards it. As they came to the houses a few people were about, but no one paid any attention to the three veiled figures. The glare of light was a sufficient indication to them of the direction they should follow, for they had

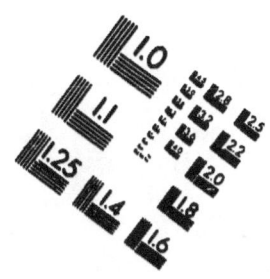

**IMAGE EVALUATION
TEST TARGET (MT-3)**

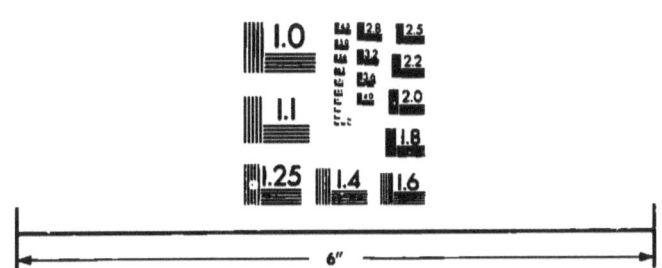

Photographic
Sciences
Corporation

23 WEST MAIN STREET
WEBSTER, N.Y. 14580
(716) 872-4503

agreed that if a landing had been made the sailors would be certain to be at work trying to put a stop to the spread of the flames.

Presently they came to the edge of the district swept by the fire. The walls for the most part were standing, although in many cases they had fallen across the road. The heaps of rubbish inside still glowed, and now and then little tongues of fire leapt up. On they went, making their way very cautiously until they reached a wide open space surrounded by ruins.

"This is the great square," Jack said. "Look, there is the fountain still playing in the middle. There are some fires there too, and a lot of people round them."

"Let us wait a bit. If they are Egyptians we shall be in a nice mess."

They stood for some time, afraid to approach closer, then they heard a burst of laughter.

"That must be English," Jack said. "I don't believe Egyptians ever laugh like that."

"I don't think so either. Let us move a bit closer; but mind, we must be ready for a bolt if we find we are wrong."

They went quietly forward, and again stood irresolute. Presently they heard a voice call "Tom Jones!" and heard the reply "Aye, aye, sir!"

"It is all right!" Jim exclaimed joyfully, and they at once hurried forward. They soon arrived at the fire, round which three or four naval officers were sitting. The boys tore the veils from their faces and threw back the cotton cloth from over their heads, and a general exclamation of surprise broke from the officers as they saw the heads of three European boys.

"Hallo!" one of them exclaimed. "Who are you, and where do you spring from?"

"We were wounded and carried off last month, on the day of the rising," Jim said, "and have been kept prisoners ever since, sir. We got away the night after the bombardment, and have just arrived. We belong to the barque *Wild Wave;* we are midshipmen on board her."

"Well, I am glad you have got out of their hands," the officer said; "but I cannot do anything for you now. These rascals keep on setting the town on fire in fresh places, and we are just starting to put one out that began half an hour ago."

"What is this?" an officer asked, hurrying up to the spot.

"Three lads, Lord Charles, who have been kept prisoners by the Egyptians for the last month, and have just escaped. They belong to a merchant vessel, and were captured at the rising."

"Please to march off your men at once, sir; I will overtake you in a minute or two. Well, lads, what can I do for you?"

"Well, sir, you might give us something to eat, perhaps," Jim suggested. "We have had next to nothing for the last three days."

"Come along with me," Lord Charles Beresford said, and he hurried with them to another party of sailors at the further end of the square.

"Give those lads something to eat and drink," he said. "You had better stop here until I come back, lads, then I will see what can be done for you."

A kettle was boiling over a fire, and before many minutes the lads were supplied with a basin each of cocoa and a lump of bread, and felt as they ate their supper that their troubles were at an end. It required, however, more than one bowl of cocoa and a considerable quantity of bread before their appetites were appeased.

While taking their supper the boys gave to the officers gathered round them a sketch of the adventures they had gone through.

"Now that you have done your supper," one of the officers said, "I suppose the next thing you want is some clothes. The question is how to get them."

"Yes, sir; it is awful going about like this."

"Well, you are rather objects," the officer agreed with a laugh; "but I do not see what is to be done for you at present. You see, all this part of the town is burned down, and the shops in the other parts are all locked up and deserted, and most of them have already been broken into and robbed. We have no time to see about that sort of thing at present; our time is entirely occupied in fighting the fire, and in preventing these scoundrels from lighting fresh ones. There were seven or eight fresh outbreaks to-day. However, you must stop here for the present. Lord Charles Beresford will not be long before he is back, I daresay."

In another half hour the party of sailors returned, having pulled down two or three houses, and prevented the flames from spreading. Their commander at once came up to the boys, followed by a sailor bringing a large bundle.

"I have not forgotten you, youngsters. One of the houses we pulled down was a clothier's, which had by some good luck or other escaped being looted, so I told the men to pick out half a dozen suits and as many caps, and bring them on. They would only have been taken by the natives directly our backs were turned. No doubt you will find something there to fit you."

With great joy the boys seized the bundle, and going a little distance off examined its contents. After a good deal of trying on they each found things that fitted them fairly. Feeling vastly more comfortable in their new attire, they rejoined the sailors.

"I expect your ship has left long ago," Lord Charles said. "Your best plan will be to go round in the morning to the consul, Mr. Cookson. He has established himself in a temporary office just beyond the range of the fire. One of my men will show you the way. Most likely your captain will have left some message with him in case you turned up again. After you have seen him you can, if you like, come back here; I daresay I shall be able to find something for you to do. Or if you like you can be sent off to one of the steamers, where the refugees are on board."

"We would much rather stay here, sir, if we may," Jim Tucker said. "We will do anything that you like to set us to."

As they sat by the fire talking with the officers the boys learned what had happened in the town. As soon as it became evident that the fire of the ships of war was mastering that of the forts the troops and the populace began the work of plunder. The European stores were all broken into;

everything portable was carried away and the furniture broken and smashed.

Fire was applied in scores of places. A considerable number of the poorer classes of Europeans had remained in their houses, being afraid to desert their possessions, and many of these houses were broken into by the mob and the inmates massacred.

It was calculated that upwards of five hundred were killed. The clerks at the Anglo-Egyptian Bank had determined to stay and defend it, and as soon as the work of plunder and massacre began a number of Europeans made for this point, and the little garrison was swelled until it numbered nearly a hundred men. The place had been attacked by the mob and soldiers; but had held out gallantly and beaten off the assailants, who had before long scattered to points where plunder could be more easily obtained.

At night a steam-launch from the fleet entered the harbour. Two or three men had landed, and making their way through the burning streets returned and reported that the town was empty.

The next morning at daylight a force had landed and driven the plunderers from the European part of the town, while the ships had battered the forts that still held out. The following day a strong force of marines came ashore and patrolled the streets. At the sight of the British uniforms many doors were opened, and the wretched inmates, who had for forty-eight hours been trembling for their lives, made their way down to the water-side and went off to the ships. In the evening, a short time before the boys arrived, four hundred and fifty men had been landed from the British ships, and one hundred and twenty-five from an American man-of-war, and these at once set about the work of re-establishing order.

In the morning a sailor conducted the boys to the house where Mr. Cookson had established himself. As soon as they gave an account of themselves to him he shook them heartily by the hand.

"I am glad to see you back in safety, lads. Your captain was in a great way about your loss, and hunted high and low for you. He traced you to the spot where the riot began, but could learn nothing more; and as none of your bodies could be found, we had hopes that you had not been killed. Of course he could not delay his vessel here, and went on to Smyrna. He was going to look in here again on his way back; but as he has not done so, he probably got a freight and had to sail straight home. He asked me if you did turn up to let you have any money you required, and to do all I could for you. I can let you have the money, but I cannot do much else beyond sending you on board one of the ships outside to wait there until there is a chance of sending you home."

"Thank you very much, sir," Jim said. "We shall be glad of some money, but we do not want to go on board ship. Lord Beresford said he would give us something to do here."

"Oh, if Lord Charles said that, I need not trouble about you," the consul said. "He will find you plenty of work. How much shall I give you each?"

"I think two pounds apiece, sir, would be plenty," Jim said. "One does not like having no money; but I do not see how we are going to spend it."

The lads now went back to the square, and there waited for some hours, Lord Charles Beresford being away at work. He returned at midday, by which time the party in the square had cooked the dinners for their comrades. There were now two thousand sailors and marines on shore, posted in various open places, the grand square serving as head-quarters. Sailors and officers were alike blackened with ashes and dust, having been engaged in the work of pulling down houses and checking the progress of the flames.

Lord Charles called the lads to him and made them sit down and join the officers and himself at dinner, and while the meal was going on he obtained from them an account of their adventures. When they had finished he said to one of the marine officers: "Captain Archer, you are to take command of that gang of fellows over there," pointing to some two hundred natives who were gathered a short distance away, "I hope we shall have a thousand at work to-morrow morning. You can take these young gentlemen with you; they will remain under your command for the present, and you will put them on rations. It will be a great thing getting these gangs of natives at work. I shall have time now to put a stop to the looting and incendiarism. Besides, they say the Egyptian troops are approaching the town again. I only hope they will try to come in."

There was a murmur of agreement among the circle of officers. The moment the meal was over the party rose, for there was no time to waste. Captain Archer, followed by the three boys and six marines, went over to the group of natives, by whom one of the dragomans of the consulate was standing

"These are all I could hire to-day, sir," the man said. "They are too much frightened to come out of their houses. To-morrow we shall get plenty of men. The consul told me to go with you as interpreter."

"Thank goodness for that," the captain said. "I was wondering how I was going to get them to understand me. Tell them to fall-in two and two and follow."

Through the streets, where the heat from the houses was so intense that they hurried through with their hands shading their faces, clambering over masses of fallen stonework, broken furniture, and goods of all sorts scattered about, the party made their way to the edge of the fire. Here the flames were ascending, and the conflagration was still spreading, although fortunately but slowly, for there was scarce any wind.

"Now, lads," the captain said, "set to work and get down four houses on each side of the way."

The marines set the example by entering the houses, and, running upstairs, soon managed to break their way through the tiles and emerge upon the roofs.

"Come on, darkies!" they shouted. "Don't be afraid of blacking your hands!" They at once began to throw off the tiles, and were soon joined by a score of the most active natives.

"That is right, down with them!" the captain shouted, and in a very few minutes the last tiles had fallen. As soon as the shower had ceased the whole of the contents of the houses were carried into the streets. Then the marines began with the axes and crowbars with which they were provided to tear up the floor-boards and break down the rafters and beams. Then grapnels fastened to long ropes were fixed on the top of the brickwork, a score of hands caught hold, and the lightly-built wall readily yielded to the strain, coming down in great masses. As soon as the walls had fallen the natives were set to work carrying away the beams and woodwork, and in a little more than half an hour from the time the operations commenced two heaps of brickwork and rubbish alone marked the spot where the eight houses had stood.

As soon as the work was finished the party moved on into the next street, there to repeat the operations. As parties of sailors were at work at a score of other places the operations proceeded rapidly, and by nightfall the workers had the satisfaction of knowing that the fire was completely cut off, and that there was no chance of its spreading farther. Four other outbreaks had occurred in the course of the day. In two cases the sailors arrived upon the spot before the incendiaries had made their escape. One man was shot, and four taken before the Egyptian magistrate who had been appointed to try cases, and they were, after their guilt had been fully proved, sentenced to death and summarily hanged.

The following evening, on their going round to the consulate as usual to hear if he had received any news of the *Wild Wave*, Mr. Cookson said, "I had a telegram an hour since, lads, saying that your ship arrived in the Thames yesterday, and asking if I had any news of you. I have sent off my answer, 'All here safe and well, making themselves useful and waiting instructions.' I am sure to get an answer some time to-morrow."

The next day the answer came, "Delighted at news. Tell boys remain Alexandria. Ship coming out with cargo coal."

CHAPTER XIV.

A SET OF RASCALS.

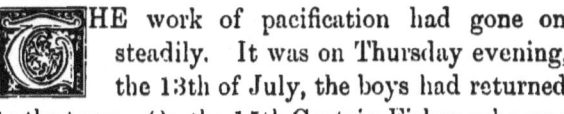HE work of pacification had gone on steadily. It was on Thursday evening, the 13th of July, the boys had returned to the town. On the 15th Captain Fisher, who was in command of the naval party on shore, marched through the streets disarming the Egyptian soldiers, of whom there were large numbers still in the place, and had a skirmish with a strong party of them at the Rosetta gate. Lord Charles Beresford was in charge of the police arrangements, and with a force of marines and three hundred disarmed Egyptian soldiers was occupied in stamping out the fires and in arresting marauders. A large number of Arabs were also enlisted in the service.

The population now began to return to the city. Many of the lower class of Greeks and Italians landed from the vessels, and were a source of continual trouble, as they at once took to plundering what the natives had left.

On Monday morning the 38th Regiment and the third battalion of the 60th Rifles arrived in the harbour, and were at once landed. General Sir Archibald Alison also arrived and assumed the command on shore, and the following day a body of troops marched along the line of railway to Ramleh, six miles distant. Ramleh stands at the point where a narrow neck of land connects the peninsula on which Alexandria stands with the mainland. Along this narrow isthmus run the road, the railway, and the Sweet-water Canal, and here there is a pumping-station, by which water is raised to a higher level for the supply of Alexandria.

The khedive has a summer palace at Ramleh, and here are a large number of pretty villas, the summer abodes of the merchants of Alexandria. It was an important position, for here any advance upon the city from the east could be readily checked.

Thursday was a busy day for the police and troops in Alexandria, for a high wind got up and fanned the masses of embers into flames again, and serious fires broke out in several places. The boys were busily engaged all day. They acted now as aides-de-camp to Lord Charles Beresford, carrying his orders to the various working parties, and making themselves generally useful.

Lord Charles had established himself with his officers in an empty house, and the three boys had a room assigned to them here. The party all messed together. In the evening Lord Charles said to the officers, "I hear that the khedive's people have got news that Arabi is damming up the Sweet-water Canal. We shall have a deal of trouble if he does. There is very bad news, too, from the country. They say that everywhere except at Cairo the natives have risen and massacred the Europeans. Arabi has ordered all the able-bodied men in the country to join the army."

"I don't call the last part bad news," Captain Archer said. "We shall have ten thousand men here in a short time, and the more of these scoundrels that are gathered together the better, so that we can end it at one blow. If Arabi does but stand there is no doubt as to the result. The thing that would puzzle us would be for him and his troops to march away into Upper Egypt and lead us a long dance there. In this tremendous heat our fellows would not be able to march far, and it would be like a tortoise trying to catch a hare, hunting them all over the country. The more men Arabi gets together the more likely he is to make a stand and fight it out."

"There is no doubt that is the case," Lord

Charles agreed. "We shall make short work of them directly Lord Wolseley and the troops arrive. However, I hope we sha'n't be idle in the meantime. There are two more regiments expected to-morrow or next day, and I expect we shall see some fighting then. The soldiers are furious at the frightful destruction that has taken place, and they will make it hot for these fellows if they get a chance of going at them. They say that they are throwing up tremendous fortifications across the isthmus."

On Sunday night the 46th Regiment arrived. The water in the canal was now sinking fast. A dam had been erected at its mouth to keep in what water it contained. Order had now been restored in the town, and the plundering had been almost put a stop to. The next morning a wing of the 60th and a squadron of mounted infantry went out beyond Ramleh. The enemy's cavalry were driven off, and there was an exchange of artillery fire between some heavy guns that had been sent out by rail and placed into position there, and Arabi's battery.

The next week was a quiet one, but on Friday the 28th a reconnaissance was made by a railway train, which Captain Fisher of the navy had plated with iron. It was manned by sailors, and carried a heavy gun and several Gatlings. The enemy on seeing it approaching came out in force, but were driven back by the guns of the train and those in the batteries at Ramleh. The reconnaissance showed that the Egyptians had erected a number of strong works across the end of the isthmus.

As the work of the bands of hired natives was now only clearing up rubbish and litter, the boys agreed that as there was no more fun to be had in the way of putting out fires, they might as well give up what they called slave-driving, and enjoy themselves until the *Wild Wave* arrived. They had only undertaken the work as an alternative to going on board one of the crowded ships in the harbour, and as the population were now returning and the shops opening again there was no occasion for their further stay as overlookers of the scavengers. Several temporary inns had been opened by enterprising Italians for the benefit of those who on landing from the ships found their houses burnt, sacked, or uninhabitable.

"I vote," Jack said the first morning that they were free to do exactly as they liked, "that we go up and have a look at our prison."

"A bright idea!" Jim Tucker said. "But that is an out-of-the-way part, Jack, and there may be some of those skulking thieves hanging about there."

"They won't catch us napping this time, Jim."

The boys had, in fact, armed themselves from the store of weapons that had been taken from the natives or found scattered about in the streets and houses. These weapons had been piled up in a shed, and as they had no owners the boys concluded that it would be as well to pick some out for themselves, having previously asked their officer to allow them to do so, as they were entirely without arms. He at once gave them permission to take what they liked, and each had taken two revolvers—a full-sized one which they wore openly in their belts, and a small one in their jacket-pockets. The precaution was by no means a useless one, as on carrying messages for their commander from one part of the town to the other they had often to pass through narrow streets. So armed the boys had no fear of being attacked when together, and after breakfast they started on their trip of exploration.

As they knew nothing of the road by which they had been taken to the house, and had again left it after nightfall, they were by no means sure as to its exact position, the only indication being the view they had obtained of the sea from its garden. When once beyond the town they found almost all the houses entirely deserted; for bands of plunderers were still pillaging everywhere beyond the range of the parties of British troops, and even after Ramleh was occupied they made their way along the shore from the direction of the Aboukir Forts, and broke into the houses and carried away their contents.

"I think this must be just about the position," Jim said at last. "I should say from the other side of that house there must be just the same view we had."

The gate was locked and closed, but the boys soon found a place where they could enter the grounds. Upon going round to the north side of the house they found that they had judged correctly, for they at once recognized the appearance of the building and the various objects in the garden.

"Here is the bank from which we watched the bombardment," Arthur Hill said. "Well, we have got better out of it than seemed likely then."

"That we have," Jack agreed. "Now, Jim, I suppose we may as well get into the house and have a look at it. I should like to get something to carry away. I don't want anything valuable, but something as a sort of memento of our prison."

"It would serve the beggar right," Jim said, "if we were to set fire to his place and burn it down."

"It might serve him right if someone else were to do it," Jack said; "but not for us, Jim. He saved our lives, you see. If it had not been for him we should never have come alive out of that street."

"That is so," Jim agreed; "but you know when we talked it over we were all of opinion that he carried us off only to act as hostages for himself."

"Well, I know we agreed that that was it, Jim; but after all we cannot be sure about it. It may have been that, but on the other hand he may really have wanted to save our lives. He would not dare treat us kindly, and was obliged to keep us imprisoned because of the fellows round him. For you know he really did treat us well. We may be sure that black fellow of his did not bring us down fruit and other things each meal without his knowledge."

"It may have been that," Jim assented, "though I doubt it. I am convinced he only carried us off and treated us well in order to get good terms for himself if things went wrong."

"Perhaps so, Jim; but whatever the reason he did save our lives, and he did treat us well, and I feel obliged to him. Now, let us look at the house. I wonder whether it is empty?"

"Oh, of course it is empty. Why, we saw all his fellows coming away with us."

"Yes, but that is no reason why it should be empty, Jim. There are lots of these plundering fellows about. We know they do not come back into the town because we have got guards at the gates, and I expect they hide up during the day in some of these deserted houses. Anyhow we may as well keep our eyes open till we know the place is clear."

Jim agreed to the prudence of the suggestion, and they went up to the house. The door opening into the garden was fastened, but the wooden shutters outside one of the windows about four feet from the ground were unfastened, and swung open as they touched them. The window inside was closed.

"Just give me a back, Arthur," Jack said. "I have no doubt I can open the fastenings."

Standing on Arthur's shoulders Jack took out his knife, and had no difficulty in inserting the blade between the frames of the window, which opened inwards, and in pushing back the slight and simple fastening. He pushed the window open, and had his foot on the sill ready to enter when he paused.

"What is it, Jack?" Jim asked impatiently.

"There is somebody in the house," Jack said in a low voice. "I can hear talking." He stepped very quietly down into the room, and a minute later the others stood beside him.

It was as Jack had said, there was a loud sound of talking somewhere in the house.

"What shall we do, Jim?" Jack whispered.

"We will go and have a look at them," Jim replied. "We have got two revolvers apiece, and are a match for a dozen Egyptians anyway; and besides, if they haven't seen us, and I don't suppose they have, as we came round at the back of the house, they will think we are officers and have got a lot of men behind us."

With their pistols drawn and cocked the boys moved quietly across the room and into a passage. The voices came from a room in the front of the house. The door was open. They crept up to it, and then suddenly rushed in.

"Surrender," Jim shouted, "or we fire!"

The lads were astonished at the sight that met their eyes. They had expected to see a group of natives; instead of that they saw a party of eight or ten Greeks and Italians sitting on the ground playing cards. The room was piled with goods of all sorts—silk curtains, female dresses, clocks, rich ornaments, choice carpets, and other articles.

The fellows uttered a shout of astonishment and dismay at seeing, as they believed, three English officers suddenly appear before them; for by this time the boys had been able to rig themselves out in naval costume again. Their appearance and that of the six levelled revolvers completely paralized the party at cards.

"Throw down all your weapons in the centre," Jack said peremptorily. "Not a moment's delay, or we will call our men in and string you up!"

Two or three of the party understood English, and at once threw their pistols and knives into the centre of the circle; the others understanding the order from their action did the same.

"Just collect them, Arthur, and take them into the next room," Jim Tucker said, "before they have time to think about it."

Arthur stepped forward, gathered up the weapons, and carried them into the next room.

"We are all right now," Jim said in a low tone. "Now, Arthur, you run down to the town as hard as you can and tell the first officer you meet we have got a gang of plunderers here, and ask him to bring up a guard and capture them; we will stand sentry till you come back."

Arthur without question obeyed Jim's orders: went to the front door, opened it, and ran off at the top of his speed. The prisoners now began to recover from the first panic, and to guess the true state of the case. Angry oaths were uttered, and they began to talk to each other in rapid tones.

"You had better sit still!" Jim shouted. "The first man that makes a move I will blow his brains out. Jack, you stand on one side of the circle and I will stand on the other. The first man who moves in the slightest, shoot him."

Jack moved round to the other side of the circle. The marauders, with a foe behind and another in front armed with revolvers, and themselves without weapons, did not dare to move, knowing that they would be shot down before they could gain their feet. Half an hour passed and then there was a tramp of feet heard outside, and a moment later a naval officer accompanied by Arthur and followed by a party of ten blue-jackets entered the room. In a couple of minutes the men's hands were all tied behind them, and they were led outside the house.

"You have made a fine haul, young gentlemen," the officer said as he walked from room to room. Everywhere articles of value were piled up, and it was evident that the gang must for the last fortnight have been engaged in looting all the villas and houses along the road to Ramleh. "I expect we have got the whole gang, but I will leave four men here in charge with orders to make prisoners of anyone that enters. We will lodge these scoundrels in jail, and then make our report. There is an immense lot of valuable property here, and I should think it had better be taken down into the town and kept there until claimed by its rightful owners."

Leaving the four sailors on guard, the party with the prisoners in their midst marched down again to the town, and the latter were speedily lodged in jail. On the affair being reported to Lord Charles Beresford a party of marines and natives with hand-carts were sent up to the house, and the whole of its contents brought down to an empty house in the town. Here the articles were inspected by many merchants and other owners of villas at Ramleh and near the town, and many of the articles were at once identified by them. The next day the band of plunderers were brought up before the court, presided over by one by the khedive's judges; and the boys having given their evidence, and the owners of many of the plundered villas swearing to their property, the whole band were sentenced to receive three dozen lashes apiece and to be imprisoned for two years.

The lads gained much credit by the capture, and were each presented with a handsome gold watch and chain, subscribed for by those whose property they had been the means of recovering.

CHAPTER XV.

A THREATENING SKY.

AT the end of July so large a number of troops had arrived that the services of the sailors on shore were no longer required, and with the exception of those serving with the iron-clad train they returned on board, the marines, however, still remaining in the town. On the 4th of August the lads heard that a reconnaissance would take place next day, and that there would probably be a fight. Accordingly in the evening they walked up to Ramleh, and slept for the night in one of the deserted houses. The trains soon began to arrive loaded with troops, and the boys took up their position near one of the batteries on the sand-hills, where they could obtain an excellent view over the isthmus between the lakes Mareotis and Aboukir.

The advance soon began; it was composed of six companies of the 60th Rifles, four companies of the 38th, and four of the 46th. These were to march by the canal, while seven companies of the marines moved along the railway embankment in company with the iron-clad train. The two parties were to join at the point where the canal and the railway approach closely to each other. The ground between the two embankments consisted of fields and marshy swamps.

The boys watched the 60th Rifles extending in skirmishing order, and as soon as they began to advance a movement was visible in the enemy's lines, and the Egyptians took up their position in a deep ditch across the line of advance and opened a heavy fire upon the Rifles.

The Egyptians were altogether invisible, their position being only marked by a light line of smoke rising in front of a thick jungle. Fortunately they fired high, and the boys could see that the Rifles continued advancing without much loss. When they neared the Egyptian position the supports came up to the skirmishing line, and the whole went forward at a rush. The instant they did so the Egyptians sprang from their ditch and rushed into the jungle behind.

The column was intended to advance to a white house on the canal, at the point where the railway came close to it; but its commander misunderstanding his orders stopped at a white house before he came to it. Thus the marines advancing along the embankment were left unsupported. They had been met with a hot fire from the enemy, who were posted in a large house surrounded by entrenchments, on which some guns had been mounted. The guns on the train kept up a steady fire on this position, and the marines pushing forward were soon hotly engaged by the enemy's infantry, who were massing in great numbers on both of their flanks.

As the marines were now far in advance of the other column, the order was given them to fall back. To cover this movement, Major Donald with fifty men advanced boldly close to the Egyptian position, and kept up so hot a fire that the enemy's advance was checked, while the main bodies of the marines retired steadily across the fields to the embankment, keeping perfect order in spite of the tremendous fire that was poured into them, and bringing off every wounded man as he fell. Major Donald's party then fell back rapidly and joined them.

The enemy had now brought up several batteries of artillery, which opened upon the marines, while the infantry pressed forward in heavy masses. The marines, however, aided by the musketry fire of the sailors in the train, as well as by their machine-guns and heavy pieces of artillery, kept them at bay as they fell back along the embankment, and as soon as the Egyptians came within range, the guns at Ramleh opened upon them, and they fell back to their camps, while the British columns returned to Ramleh.

The object of the reconnaissance had been served by the discovery of the strength and position of the enemy's batteries, and it was evident that it would need a large force to carry the formidable positions which guarded the isthmus.

A week later the lads, on paying their usual morning visit to the consulate, heard to their delight that the *Wild Wave* had just been signalled approaching the harbour, which was now crowded with shipping, as steamers laden with troops were arriving every day from England. The lads hurried down to the port, and as soon as the *Wild Wave* dropped her anchor they were alongside of her. They were very warmly greeted by the captain and officers as they came on board ship.

"Well, you young scamps," Captain Murchison said after the first greetings were over, "you have given us a nice fright. What has it all been about? for at present we have heard nothing whatever beyond the fact that you were safe; and we are prepared to put you in irons for desertion unless you can give us a completely satisfactory explanation of your absence. Mr. Timmins and myself are strongly of opinion that you simply hid yourselves till the vessel sailed, so as to be able to have a run on shore and see all that was going on."

"We are very glad we have seen it, sir," Jim said; "but I don't think it was at all our fault that we were left behind." And he then proceeded to relate to the captain the story of what had befallen them since they last met.

"Well, lads, I congratulate you on your escape, which was certainly a very narrow one. You have, I hope, all written to your friends at home to tell them everything that has taken place. It was most fortunate that your telegram from here arrived the day after we got to England, so that your friends practically received the news that you were missing and that you were safe at the same time. We had delayed sending off letters telling them that you were lost until we could receive an answer to our telegram to the consul. I went over and saw your mother and sister the same evening, Jack. Of course your mother was in some alarm at the thought of the danger she pictured to herself that you must have gone through. I told her I expected that when the row began you had hid up somewhere, and that not knowing that matters had quieted down again you had remained there until after we sailed."

The boys had all written home on the day after they had rejoined their friends in Alexandria, and had, a week before the arrival of the *Wild Wave*, received answers to their letters. An hour later an officer came off with orders that the coal was not to be discharged on shore, but that the transports would come alongside and fill up from her. For a week all hands were engaged in the unpleasant duty of discharging the coal. Steamer after steamer came alongside and took from one to three hundred tons on board, to supply the place of the coal consumed on the outward voyage. All on board were heartily glad when the work was over, the decks scrubbed and washed down, and the hose at work upon the bulwarks and rigging.

"We shall not be clean again till we have had twelve hour's rain on her," Captain Murchison said. "It is the first time so far as I know that the *Wild Wave* has carried coal, and I hope it will be the last, so long as I command her."

"Yes, I have been feeling a good deal like a chimney-sweep for the last week, sir," Mr. Timmins remarked; "and shall not feel clean again till all my togs have been ashore and had a regular wash."

"I shall be glad to be out of this harbour," the captain said. "These tideless harbours soon get very unpleasant when there is much shipping in them. And yet I own I should like to wait to see the attack on the Egyptain position. I believe the last transports came in to-day, and as Lord Wolseley arrived two days ago, I suppose they will be at it in a day or two. However, as I sent off a telegram this morning saying that we were empty, I suppose we shall get orders this afternoon or to-morrow morning to go somewhere."

Late in the afternoon they were surprised by seeing the boats of the fleet and transports occupied in re-embarking large numbers of troops.

"Something is evidently up," Mr. Hoare said, as he stood with the lads watching the busy scene. "I suppose Lord Wolseley thinks it will cost too many lives to attack the Egyptian position in front, and that he is going to make a fresh landing somewhere along the coast so as to march round and take them in the rear. Or it may be he is going to sail up the canal and land at Ismailia; in that way, if he is sharp, he may get between Arabi and Cairo, and cut the enemy off altogether from the capital."

The next morning at daybreak the great fleet of men-of-war and transports steamed away for the East on their way to Ismailia, and the *Wild Wave*, which had got her orders late the evening before, sailed for Genoa, where she was to take on board a cargo for England. Six weeks later she entered St. Katherine's Docks, and the three midshipmen were at once released from duty. Jack had already packed up his small kit, and, taking the train to Fenchurch and then a bus to Dulwich, was soon home. As the ship had been signalled when she passed the Downs, he was expected, and received a joyous welcome. Great was the interest of his mother and sister in the adventures he had passed through, and they were delighted with the gold watch and the inscription, stating that it had been presented to him by merchants of Alexandria whose property he had been the means of rescuing from its plunderers.

The next morning Mrs. Robson received a note asking her to come up with Jack and Lily to dine with the Godstones. Jack learned that while he had been away Lily had been often there spending the day with Mildred, who was nearly her own age. On their arrival Mildred took her off to her own room to have tea, while Jack dined with Mr. Godstone and his wife, and after dinner had again to repeat the full story of his adventures. His stay in England was a short one, for the

Wild Wave, as soon as she had unloaded her cargo from Italy, was chartered for Calcutta, via the Cape, and a fortnight after his arrival at home Jack was again summoned to rejoin his ship.

The *Wild Wave* was again fortunate in her weather during the early part of her voyage, but when off the Cape encountered a heavy gale. Jack had never before seen a storm at sea, and, accustomed as he was to the short choppy waves at the mouth of the Thames, he was astonished at the size of those he now beheld. They seemed to him as large in comparison to the size of the barque as those he had before seen were to that of the smack. For three days the vessel lay to. Fortunately the glass had given notice of the approach of the storm, and all the upper spars had been sent down and the vessel got under snug canvas before it struck her, and she therefore rode out the gale with no farther damage than the carrying away of part of her bulwarks, and the loss of some hen-coops and various other of her deck gear. As soon as the gale abated sail was made, and they continued on their course.

"Glad it is over, eh, Master Robson?" the sail-maker, Joe Culver, said to Jack as he was leaning against the bulwark on the evening after the storm had subsided, looking at the reflection of the setting sun on the glassy slopes of the long swell that was still heaving. Joe Culver, or, as he was always called on board, Old Joe, was a character; he had sailed as man and boy over fifty-five years on board ships belonging to the firm; and now, although sixty-seven years old, was still active and hearty. It was a legend among the sailors that Old Joe had not changed in the slightest degree from the time he was entered in the ship's books as a boy.

"Old Joe is like the figure-head of a ship," a sailor said one day. "He got carved out of wood when he was little; and though he has got dinted about a bit, he ain't never changed nothing to speak of. If you could but paint him up a bit he would be as good as new."

Joe could have gone into quarters on shore with a pension years before, for his long service had made him a marked character; and while other sailors came and went in the service of the firm, the fact that his name had been on their books for so long a period, with but two breaks, had made him a sort of historical character, and at the end of each long voyage he was always expected to show himself at the office to have a few words with the head of the firm. He was still rated as an able seaman, with extra pay as sailmaker, but he was never expected to go aloft.

In every other respect he could still do his work, and could turn out a new sail or alter an old one as well as any sailmaker on board Mr. Godstone's fleet.

As Captain Murchison remarked to the owners when he saw that Joe was this voyage to form one of his crew: "The old fellow would be worth his pay if he never put his hand to work. He keeps a crew in good humour with his yarns and stories; and if there is a grumbler on board he always manages to turn the laugh against him, and to show him to the others in his true light as a skulker and a sneak. He looks after the boys and puts them up to their duty, and acts generally as a father to them. A man like that, attached to the owners, always cheerful and good-tempered, ready to make the best of everything, and to do his work to the best of his power, is a very valuable man on board a ship. I always feel that things will go on comfortably forward when I see Joe Culver's name down in the articles."

"It was grand, Joe," Jack replied in answer to his question, "though it was very awful. I had no idea that a storm would be anything like that, or the waves so high. I have seen storms on our own East Coast, and they seemed bad enough, but they were nothing to this."

" And this weren't nothing to some storms I have seen in these latitudes, Master Robson. I have doubled the Cape two score of times, I should say --eh, more than that, coming and going—and I have seen storms here to which that which has just blown over was but a capful of wind. Why, sir, I have seen a ship laid on her beam-ends when she was not showing a rag of canvas, and even when we had cut all the masts away the pressure of wind on her hull kept her down until we thought that she would never right again. Altogether I have been wrecked eight times, and three of them was down in these ere latitudes. They says as my name has been on the books of the firm for fifty-five years; but that ain't quite correct, for twice it was written off with D.D. after it, but somehow or other I turned up again, just as you see. One of these 'ere businesses happened hereabouts."

"I should like to hear about it awfully, Joe."

"Well, sir, seeing it was not what you may call an everyday sort of affair, and as perhaps the yarn might give you a hint as might be useful to you if you ever gets into the same kind of fix, I don't mind if I tell you. Just at present I have not finished my work, but if you and the other two young gents like to come forward here at six bells I will tell you about it."

CHAPTER XVI.

OLD JOE'S YARN.

AT seven o'clock the three lads gathered round the old sailor forward. Joe having got his pipe to draw to his satisfaction, proceeded to relate the story of his shipwreck.

"It happened," he said, "on the very first v'yage I made as an A.B.; and proud I was, as you may guess, that I had done at last with being ordered here and ordered there, and kicked here and cuffed there. I was just twenty-one then, and as active and hearty a young chap as you would want to see; not over big, you know, and spare in flesh, but as strong and active as any on board a ship. Well, it came on to blow just about the same latitude where the storm struck us the other day, but much heavier. I never saw a worse sky in all my v'yges, and when the blow came it seemed to me there was an end of everything at once. I need not tell you about the storm; you just take the last one and pile it up about ten times, and you have got it.

"Although we were ready and prepared for it, and had snugged down till we scarce showed a rag of sail, over she went at the first blow, till we all thought as she was going to turn turtle. We cut away her main and mizzen, and at last got her before it and run. That gale blew for ten days right on end. The sea was tremendous. Over and over again we were pooped, our bulwarks were carried away, the boats smashed, the caboose and pretty nigh everything else on deck swept clean off. Five of the hands had been washed overboard, another three men were down below badly hurt, and the first-mate had his leg broke. We were all pretty well exhausted, as you may guess. Where we'd got to none knew, for we had never had a glimpse of the sun since the gale began; and it would not have made much difference if we had, because, you see, we could do nothing but just run before the wind wherever it liked to take us. But we knew anyhow we had got down into high latitudes, for the gale had been blowing pretty steady from the north-west.

"The air got bitterly cold all of a sudden; and though we could not see above a mile anywhere round us, we were pretty sure we were in the neighbourhood of ice. Towards the afternoon of the tenth day the weather cleared just a little, though the wind seemed as high as ever, and we caught sight of some big bergs. The captain, who was as good a sort as ever sailed, had done his best all along to keep up our spirits. The cook had been washed overboard in his caboose; but the skipper had kept his steward at work boiling water over a little spirit-stove he had aft, and kept a supply of hot coffee there at all hours for us; and with that and biscuits we had got on fairly well. Now he told us that he thought the gale would soon blow itself out, and that as soon as it abated enough to set a rag or two of sail he would try and bring us up under the lee of a berg.

"But it wasn't to be. It had just struck four bells, and there was a gleam of daylight; I was at the helm, with the captain, who had never laid down for above an hour at a time since the gale began, beside me. Suddenly I saw it become lighter ahead, just like a gray shadow against the blackness. I had but just noticed it when the skipper cried out, 'Good God! there is a berg straight ahead, it is all over with us!' and then he gave a shout, 'All hands on deck!'

"'There was nothing to do. We could not have changed our course a point if we had tried ever so much, and the berg, as we could see in another minute, stretched right away on both sides of us.

"'You can leave the helm, Joe,' says the skipper; 'we have done all that men could do, we are in God's hands now.' I went forward with the rest, for I knew well as the only chance was to get on to the berg when she struck. It did not seem much of a chance, but it is wonderful how one clings to the hope of a few hours more life.

"It was not five minutes from the time when we first saw the gray shadow ahead that we struck. The crash was tremendous. The mast snapped off as if it was a pipe-stem. The whole front of the ship seemed stove in, and I believe that more than half of those gathered forward were killed, either by the fall of the mast or by the breaking up of the bows. The bowsprit was driven aft through the bits against the stump of the foremast, and did its share in the work. I was standing in the fore-chains, having got over there to avoid the fall of the mast. Though I was holding tight to the shrouds I was well-nigh wrenched from my hold. There was one terrible cry, and then the ship seemed to break up as if she were glass, and I was in the water. A great wave came thundering down on me; it seemed to me as if I was being carried right up into the air, then I felt a shock, and it was sometime before I knew anything more.

"When I came to myself it was daylight. For a bit I could not move, and I thought my ribs were staved in; but at last, after much trouble, I made a shift to work myself out and found that I was about fifty feet above the water. The wave had carried me upon its crest as it swept up the face of the berg, and just as it was at its highest had, by God's mercy, jammed me in between two pinnacles of ice, and though I daresay others had swept up as high, none of them had moved me. I sat for a time dazed and stupid, and then began to take a view of my position. The ship was gone. There was not a sign of a bit of floating timber or of any of my messmates. I suppose all the wreckage had been swept away by the current.

"The iceberg had, I reckon, been floating a long time, for it was seamed all over with cracks and crevices. It had been up under a pretty hot sun before the long gale blew it and us south, and the surface was rough and honey-combed. I did not feel as grateful as I ought to have done, lads, that I had been cast up, for I saw nothing but death before me; and thought that it would have been better to have died when I lost my senses in the water than to have to die again as it were by cold or hunger on the berg. However I set-to to climb over the berg and down to the other side so as to get under its lee. It took me two or three hours of hard work, but by the end of that time my clothes were dry, and I got some spirit and hope in me again.

"Once over there I was pretty comfortable; the berg sheltered me from the wind, and the sun began to shine out a bit through the clouds, and in the afternoon, although it was still blowing hard, there was a blue sky overhead. There were a good many other bergs in sight, but none of them seemed near as big as the one that I was on. Fortunately I had a couple of biscuits in my pocket, having thrust them in there when I run up when there was a call for an extra hand at the helm. One of these I ate, then I lay down on a broad ledge and went off sound asleep. When I awoke it was night. I was warmly clad when we struck, having my thick oil-skin over my pea-jacket, but I felt a bit cold. However I was soon off again, and when I awoke morning had broken. I ate half my last biscuit, took a drink out of a pool—I do not know whether it was melted ice or rain-water—and then climbed up to the top of the berg and looked round.

"I had not expected to see a sail, and I didn't, for we were far out of the track of ships. Still it was just possible one might have been driven south as we had been. The wind had pretty well dropped now, and the sea was going down. I could see by some small bergs near us that we were driving through the waters at a good rate. When a great mountain of ice like that, you know, gets way on it, it will keep it for a mighty long time. It did not make much difference to me which way we were going; I had only half a biscuit left, and no chance of getting more. I sat down and wondered how long I should last, and whether it would not be easier to go down and jump off into the water than to sit there and die by inches. As I was thinking, I was looking at what I had taken for another big berg, away in the distance, right on the course we were making, and it suddenly came to me that it was not the same colour as the others. I looked up to see if there was a bit of a cloud anywhere about that might have thrown it into shadow, but there weren't, and at last I felt sure that it wasn't no iceberg at all, but an island.

"I jumped on my feet now quick enough. An island would be better than this berg anyhow. There might be shell-fish and fruit—though fruit did not seem likely so far south—and birds

and seals. I had heard tales from others as to
islands in the South Seas, and though I knew
well enough that I should not find cocoa-nuts
and such like, I thought I might get hold of
something with which to make a shift to hold on
until some whaler happened to pass along. For
an hour or two I stood watching; at the end of
that time I was sure it was land, and also that
we were driving pretty straight towards it. As
we got near I could see it was a big island that
stretched right across our course, but was still a
long way off. I felt sure we should ground somewhere in the night, for I had heard that icebergs
drew a tremendous lot of water, and were two or
three times as deep below the surface as they were
above it. We were two or three hundred feet
high, so unless the water kept deep right up to the
island we should take ground a good way off it.

"When it got dark I went down on the other
side of the berg, for I had sense enough to know
that just in the same way as the masts of a ship
went straight forward when she struck, the pinnacles of the berg would go toppling down towards
the island when she grounded. I was hungry
enough, I can tell you, that day, but I kept my
last half-biscuit until the morning, so as to give
me strength to swim. I dosed off for a bit, but

about eight bells, as near as I can guess, I heard a deep grating sort of noise. Then I felt myself rising up. I went higher and higher, till I began to wonder whether there was any chance of the berg turning over. There was a noise like thunder as the pieces of ice broke off and went crashing down the other side. Then slowly I began to sink down again, and I should say for an hour the berg rolled up and down. Then I went off to sleep.

"As you may guess, I was on the top of the berg at daybreak, and saw we had drifted into a big bay, and had grounded about midway. The cliffs in most places rose sheer up out of the water, but here and there there were breaks, and I could see that the land beyond was rough and desolate-looking. I ate my last half-biscuit, and then made my way down to the water's edge. The shore seemed to me about half a mile away— a longish swim in cold water; but I was a good swimmer, and the sea between the berg and the land was as smooth as a pond. I took off my clothes, put them in the middle of my oilskin, and wrapped it round them, tying one of my stockings round the neck of the bag to keep it all together. I had bought the oilskin just before I started on that voyage, and knew that it would keep out the water tidy. I could not get down nearer than twenty feet of the sea, so I dropped the bag in and then jumped.

"As I had hoped, the thing floated light. I pushed it before me as I swam, and found that by putting my hands on it it would keep me up well when I wanted to rest. However, I did not want much of that. The water was too cold to be idle in, and I never stopped swimming until I got to shore at the point I had marked out as easiest to land on. I wasn't long opening the bag and getting into my things, which were perfectly dry. My first thought was of food. While I had been swimming I thought I heard a sort of barking noise, and I wasn't long in seeing that there were a lot of seals on the rocks. I picked up a goodish chunk of stone, and then lay down and set to crawling towards them. I had heard from sailors who had been whaling that the way to kill a seal was to hit him on the nose, and I kept this in my mind as I crawled up. They did not seem to notice me, and I got close among them without their moving. Then I jumped up. There was a young seal lying not ten feet from me, and before he had time to turn I smashed down my bit of rock between his eyes, and there he lay dead.

"Raw seal's flesh ain't a sort of food as you

would take for choice, but I was too hungry to think about cooking, and I ate as big a meal as ever I had in my life. Up till then I hadn't really thought as there was any chance of my being saved in the long run. Now I felt as there was, and for the first time I felt really grateful that I had not shared in the fate of my messmates, and I knelt down and thanked God for having brought me safe to shore. Then I set-to to climb up to the top of the cliffs. It was hard work, and, as I afterwards found, I had just hit, by God's mercy, on the only spot on that part of the island where I could have got up, for in most places the cliffs rose pretty near straight up four or five hundred feet above the sea.

"When I got to the top I saw that there were some mighty high hills covered with snow to the south-east, which might have been fifteen or twenty miles away. It was a dreary kind of country—rocky and desolate, with tufts of thin grass growing in the crevices of the rocks; and I saw that there was precious little chance of picking up a living there, and that if I was to get grub it was to the sea I must look for it. I thought the best thing to do was to try and find out some sheltered sort of cove where, perhaps, I might find a bit of a cave, for I knew that when winter came on there would not be no chance for me in the open; so I set out to walk. I brought up with me a big hunk of flesh that would last me for three or four days, and what I had got to look for was fresh water. I walked all that day, keeping along pretty close to the edge of the cliff. I found plenty of little pools of rain-water among the rocks, and did pretty well. I was not hungry enough to tackle raw flesh that night, and had nothing to make a fire with. I had got matches in my pocket in a tight-fitting brass box which had kept them dry, but there was no fuel.

"The next morning I started again, and after walking for four or five hours came to a spot where the cliffs broke away sudden. Getting to the edge I saw that there was a narrow bay stretching some way up into the island. An hour's walk brought me to its head. Here, as I had hoped, I found a little stream running down into it. When you find a bay, most times you will find water running in at its head. The ground sloped gradually here in great terraces; the rock was hard and black, and looked as if it had been burnt. I have heard since that it was what they call volcanic. Being so sheltered there were more things growing here, wherever a little earth had gathered; and I saw some things for all the world like cabbages, and made up my mind to try them, when I got a chance, with my seal-meat.

"At last I got down near the water. Just at the head of the bay was a shelving shore, and along at the sides, as far as I could see it was rocky, and there were plenty of seals here too. Along on the beach and on the rock and on the terraces were quantities of birds—penguins, as I knew from what I had heard of them. They did not try to get out of my way, but just made an angry sort of noise. 'I will talk to you presently, my hearties,' I said; 'what I have got to do now is to look for a shelter.' It was the end of April, and I knew that it would not be long before winter would be upon me, and if I was not out of it by that time I should soon be frozen still. I did not go near the seals, for I did not want to frighten them. I looked about the rest of that afternoon and all next day, but I could not find what you might properly call a cave, and so determined to make use of the best place I could fix upon. This was a spot in the lower terrace, in the face of the rock. It seemed as if the lower part was softer than the upper, which was black and hard and almost like glass. Underneath this the rock had crumbled away perhaps six feet in depth.

"This soft rock was about four feet thick. It

was more gone in some places than others. I chose a spot where a hole was about eight feet long, and made up my mind to close up the front of this, just leaving a hole big enough for me to crawl in and out. First of all I brought up some big stones and built a wall and filled up the crevices with tufts of grass. Then I brought up smaller stones and piled against them, shooting in sand from the beach till I had made a regular solid bank, four feet thick, against the wall. Then I levelled the bottom of the cave with sand and spread it thickly with dried grass. All this took me five days' hard work. There was no difficulty about food. I had only to go and pick up a few stones and go among the penguins and knock them over. I made a shift to cook them over fires made of dry tufts of grass.

"I had been careful not to disturb the seals. I did not want any of them until the weather got cold enough to freeze their flesh. I thought of oil from their blubber, but I had nothing to hold it. When I had finished my hut I began to hunt about to see if I could find drift-wood, but I could only find a few pieces in the cove, and gave it up, for I did not see how I could anyhow keep up a fire through the winter. Then I bethought me that the penguins could furnish me with feathers, and I set to work at them with earnest, and in a week had filled my cave two feet deep with feathers.

"Every day I could feel that it got colder, and at night there was a sharp frost; so I determined now to set-to at the seals. There were none of the sort that you get fur from, and there was not much warmth to be had from the skins, still they would do to block up the entrance to my den. I killed five or six of them, and found that some of the young ones were furry enough to make coats of. As I was sitting on the ground by them next morning, lamenting I had nothing to boil down their blubber in, an idea struck me. I might use the blubber as candles, sticking wicks into it. I set to work and stripped the blubber off all the seals, and cut it in squares of about six inches. Then I got a bit of one of the fresh skins, bent it up all round, of the right size for the squares to fit into, fastened it, and spread it on the rocks to dry. The thought of how I was to make wicks bothered me. I could not spare my clothes. At last, after trying different things, I found that some of the grass was very tough. I put a bundle of this in a pool, and let it lay there for a week; for I was a North of Ireland boy, and knew how they worked flax. At the end of that time I took it out, let it dry, and then bruised it between flat stones, and found that it had a tough fibre. I thanked God, and picked a lot more of it and put it to soak. You may guess I tried the experiment that night; I made six big wicks and put them in one of the cakes of blubber and lighted them, and found that they burned famously and gave out a lot of heat. I killed some more seals; and by the time the winter set in in earnest I had a stock of meat enough to last me for months, and two or three hundredweight of cakes of blubber.

"I had made several bowls and plates out of the seals' skins, and had fashioned myself, in a mighty rough way, some suits of young seal-skins with a hood that covered all my head and face except just my mouth and eyes. From the first I had eaten the cabbages regular with my food. I could not cook them, because I had nothing to boil the water in, and they were rather bitter to eat raw; but they were better than nothing with the flesh, and I knew that I must eat green food if I wanted to keep healthy. Among the drift-wood I had luckily found a couple of broken oars. To these I had fastened with seal sinews two sharp and strong bones, and they made very fair spears.

"By the end of May the ground was covered deep with snow, and the cold set in bitter. What had bothered me most of all was where I was to store my stock of frozen meat and blubber. I knew that there was a chance of bears coming, and that they would scent it out however I might hide it. At last I determined to put it in a hole something like that I had made into a den for myself. This hole was not like mine, on a level with the ground, but was on the face of a smooth cliff about forty feet high. I made a rope of seal-skin, fastened it to a projection in the rock over the hole, and lowered myself down. I found the place would do well, and was quite big enough for all my store, while the face of the rock was too steep to climb, even for a bear. So I carried all my stock up to the top, and climbing up and down the rope, stored it in the hole, except what I wanted for a week's consumption.

"Well, lads, I passed the winter there. However cold it was outside—and I can tell you it was bitter—it was warm enough in my den. At the very coldest time I had two of my lamps burning, but most of the time one kept it warm enough. I used to nestle down in the feathers and had a seal-skin over me; and however hard it blew outside, and however hard it froze, I was warm there. I used to frizzle my meat over the lamp, and every day, when the weather permitted, I went out and brought in a stock of the cabbages. I always kept a good stock of blubber in the der and several bundles of my wicks.

One night I heard a sound of snuffing outside my cave, and knew at once that the bears had come. I had thought over what I should do, and was ready for them. The hole through the bank into the cave was only big enough for me to crawl through, and I knew a bear could not come in till he had scraped it a good bit bigger. I tied a bunch of the flax to the end of one of my spears, poured a little melted grease from the lamp over it, and then drew aside the seal-skin over the entrance and peeped out.

"It was a moonlight night, and I could see a big head trying to thrust itself in at the other end of the hole. A moment later he began to scrape away at the sides. I lit the bundle of flax. It flared up fiercely, and I thrust it out full into the beast's face. He gave a roar, and off he went as fast as his feet would carry him. They tried it a dozen times if they did it once; but the torch was too much for them, and the seal bone in its middle must have given them some nasty wounds, for I generally saw blood on the snow in the morning. Whenever I went to get a fresh store of meat and blubber I could see how they had trampled on the snow at the foot of the rock, and how they had scratched its face in trying to get up at it, but it were not no manner of good. I was chased two or three times by them when I went out to gather my cabbages, but I always managed to get into my hole before they overtook me, and they had learned to give that a wide berth.

"It seemed to me as that winter was never going to be over; but I was young and had good spirits and was fond of a song, and I used to lie there and sing by the hour. Then I used to go over in my mind all the v'yges I had made and to remember the yarns I had heard, and would go over the talks I had had with Jack and Tom and Harry. You would be surprised how I kept my spirits up. You see I was a young fellow, and young fellows take things cheerful and make light of what would break them down when they get older. I never had a day's illness, which I set down to them cabbages. I never seen them anywhere else, and I larnt arterwards that Kerguelen Island—for that was the place I was thrown on —was famous for them.

"When spring came and the snow melted I made up a package of forty pounds of meat, for the seals had not come yet, and started to make a tour of the island. I thought such a place as this was pretty well sure to be used by whalers in summer; and if so, I should find signs of their having been there. I made a few excursions first, and found I was pretty near the middle of the island—of course on the westerly side. I climbed a high hill, but I did not learn much except that the island was a big one, and there were hills both to the north and south that looked to me as if they must be thirty or forty miles away. As far as I could see of the west coast of the island the cliffs were everywhere precipitous; and though at the east they did not seem much better, I concluded to try that first. You see at this point the island was not more than fifteen miles across, but it seemed to bulge out both ways, and where I was looked like a sort of neck connecting two big islands. It was an awful country to traverse, all hill and rock; but after three weeks' tramping I gave a shout, for in a bay in front of me was a large hut.

"I had had a hard time of it and was pretty well done up. My meat had lasted me well enough on short rations and I had filled up on cabbages; but I was often a long time without water, having to depend entirely on melted snow in the hollows of the rocks. I hurried down to the hut; it was a rough shed evidently erected for the use of whalers, and round it were ashes of fires, empty meat-tins, and other signs of the stay of sailors here. For the next month I lived here. The birds were returning. There was a stream close at hand, and enough drift-wood on the shores to enable me to keep up a constant fire. I woke up one morning in November to see a vessel entering the bay. The crew would scarce believe me when I told them that I passed the winter on the island alone, and that I had lived for six months on seal-meat, penguins, and cabbages. I learned from them that the bay was known as Hillsborough Bay, and the cove where the whaler entered as Betsy Cove, and that it was a regular rendezvous of whalers. I fished with them all through the summer, and went home in the ship, and was soon down again on the books of Godstone & Son."

"Well, that was a go, and no mistake, Joe!" Jim Tucker said. "Fancy having to live for six months on seal frizzled over a lamp and raw cabbages! You did not tell us how you did for drink."

"Melted snow," Joe replied. "I used to fix one of the basins of dried seal-skin a foot or so above the lamp, so that it would be hot enough to melt the snow without a risk of its burning itself. Then I used to pour the water from one basin to another for half an hour. Melted snow-water is poor stuff if you don't do that. I do not know the rights of it, but I have heard tell that it's 'cause there ain't no air in it, though for my part I never could see no air in water, except in surf. I had heard that that was the way they treated condensed water, and anyhow it was a sort of amusement like, and helped to pass the time."

"Well, it is a capital story to listen to, Joe," Jack said; "but I should not like to go through it myself. It must have been an awful time, shut up in a hole with a stinking lamp, for I expect it did stink, all those months."

"It did use to smell powerful strong sometimes, lad, and many a time at first it turned me as sick as a youngster on his first v'yage; but I got accustomed to it after a bit. The great thing was to keep your wick short."

"And now about your other wreck not far from here?"

"I will tell you that to-morrow evening, lads. That were a more ordinary kind of thing. It weren't pleasant; I don't know that wrecks ever are, but it weren't such an out-of-the-way thing as being chucked up on to an iceberg."

CHAPTER XVII.

IN DANGEROUS SEAS.

HE following evening, as the twilight was falling, the lads again gathered round the old sailor.

"Well, lads," he began, "just as this other affair I was telling you about happened further down south, so the other was a goodish bit to the north. We was bound for the Persian Gulf, and I fancy the captain got wrong with his reckonings. He had had trouble before we sailed; had lost his wife sudden, I heard, and, more's the pity, he took to drink. He was the first and last captain as ever I sailed under as did it; for Godstone & Son were always mighty particular with their masters, and would not have a man, not for ever so, who was given to lifting his elbow. Anyhow, we went wrong; and it is a baddish place to go wrong, I can tell you, is the Mozambique Channel. There was a haze on the water and a light breeze, and just about eight bells in the morning we went plump ashore—though none of us thought we were within a hundred miles of land. There was a pretty to-do, as you might fancy; but we had to wait until morning to see where we were; then we found, when the mist lifted a bit that we were on a low sandy coast.

"We had no doubt that we should get her off; so we got the boats out and the hatches off, and began to get up the cargo. We worked hard all day, and thought we had got pretty well enough out of her, and were just going to knock off work and carry out a couple of anchors and cables astern to try and heave her off, when there was a yell, and two or three hundred black fellows came dashing down on us with spears. They crept up so close before they showed, that we had no time to tumble into the boats before they were upon us. We made the best sort of fight we could, but that wasn't much. We had brought ashore muskets and cutlasses, but they had been left in the boats, and only a few of us had time to get hold of them before they were upon us. I cut and slashed as well as I could, but it was not for long; for a spear lodged in my shoulder just at the moment when a big native caught me a clip over the head with a club, and down I went.

"I fancy I was some time before I got my senses again. When I did I found that I was tied hand and foot, and was lying there on the sands, with three or four of our fellows in the same plight as myself. They all belonged to the jolly-boat in which I had come ashore. The other boat had made a shift to push off with some of its hands and get back to the ship; but I did not know that until afterwards, for I was lying down behind a hillock of sand and could not get a view of the sea. There were lots of natives about, and they seemed mighty excited. I could hear a dropping fire of muskets, and guessed that those on board was keeping up a fire on any who so showed themselves on the beach. The natives got more and more excited, and kept jabbering together and pointing away along the coast; and I guessed that some of their own craft were coming to attack the ship.

"Presently I heard one of the guns, then another and another. The shot didn't come whistling our way, so I had no doubt that the ship was attacked. For a quarter of an hour the firing went on—cannon and musketry. I could hear the yells of the natives and the shouts of our men, though I could see nothing. The natives round me were pretty near out of their minds with excitement; then they began to dance and yell, and all at once the firing ceased, and I knew that the niggers had taken the ship. I was afraid it would come to that; for you see they had lost pretty well a third of their crew in the fight on shore, and the niggers would never have ventured to attack if they had not been ten to one against them.

"We lay there all that night, and I believe I should have died of thirst if a nigger wench had not taken compassion on us and given us a drink. The next morning our ropes were undone. Our first look when we got up was natural towards the ship. There she lay, with a dozen native craft round her. Her decks were black with niggers, and they were hard at work stripping her. No one paid much attention to us, for there was nowhere we could run to; and we sat down together and talked over our chances. We saw nothing of our shipmates; and whether they were all killed, or whether some of them were put aboard the native craft, I never knew. They were some days unloading and stripping the ship, and they had big quarrels over the division of the spoil. I think the fellows with boats did our natives out of their share, beyond what fell into their hands when they first attacked us. However, at last it was all done; then two chiefs came and had a look at us, and one took me and Tom Longstaff, and another took the other two.

"We had not done bad for eating while we were on shore, for there was several barrels of pork and biscuits among the lot we had landed, and we were free to take as much as we wanted. The other bales and boxes were all broken open and the contents made up into packets, and Tom and I and about sixty niggers, each with as much as he could stagger under, started away from the shore. It wasn't a long march, for their village lay only about six miles away. We knew it could not be far, because the women and children had come down to the beach two or three hours after the fight was over. We stopped here about a month, and then one morning the chief and four of his men started off with Tom and me. We made three days' marches, such marches as I never want to do again. Tom and I did our best to keep up; but the last day we was quite worn out, and if it hadn't been that they thumped us with their spears and prodded us up, we should never have done it.

"The place we got to was a deal bigger than the first village. We were left outside the biggest hut with the four fellows to guard us, while the chief went inside. Presently he came out again with a chap quite different to himself. He was brown instead of being black, and dressed quite different; and having been trading up in the Persian Gulf I knew him to be an Arab. He looked us over as if we had been bullocks he intended to buy, and then went into the hut again. A few minutes later our chief came out and made signs to us that we belonged to the Arab now, and then went away with his men, and we never saw him again. We had an easy time of it for the next week, and then the Arab started with a number of carriers laden with goods for the interior.

"You would scarcely believe, lads, what we went through on that 'ere journey. Many a time Tom and me made up our minds to bolt for it; and we would have done it if we had had the least idee which way to go or how we were to keep alive on the journey. We had agreed when we started that we would do our best, and that we would not put up with no flogging. We didn't much care whether they killed us or not, for we would just as leave have died as passed our lives in that country with all its beastly ways. Well, a couple of days after we had started, a big nigger driver who had been laying on his stick freely on the backs of the slaves came along, and let Tom and me have one a-piece. Tom, who was nearest to him, chucked down his load and went right at him, and knocked him over like a ninepin.

"Well, some of the other drivers or guards, or whatever they call them, ran up, and there was a tidy skrimage, I can tell you. It was ten minutes, I should say, before they got the best of us; and there was not one among them but was badly damaged about the figure-head. When they had got us down they laid it on to rights, and I believe they would have finished us if the Arab had not come up and stopped it.

"'Look here,' says I, when I was able to get up on to my feet again; 'we are ready to work just as far as men can work, but if one of them niggers lays a finger on us we will do for him. You may cut us in pieces afterwards, but we will do for him.'

"I don't know whether the Arab understood just what I said, but I think he got the gist of it. He spoke sharp to his men, and they never touched us afterwards. I could not quite make out what they were taking us for, because I can say honest as we were not much good at carrying —not half as good as one of the slaves. The first

day or two we carried a good manful load. Then
our shoes went to pieces, and we got that footsore
and bad we could scarcely crawl along, let alone
carrying loads. Tom said as he thought as the
Arab was a-taking us to sell as curios to some
fellow who had never seen white men before, and
it turned out as he was right. After we had been
travelling for nigh a month we came to a big
village; and there was great excitement over our
coming, and for two days there was feastings,
while the Arab sold part of his goods to the
people for gold dust and ivory.

"The chief had come to look at us the day we
arrived, and we had been packed away together
in a little hut. The third day he came again
with the Arab, and made signs that I was his property now, while the Arab told Tom to go out
and start with his caravan. It was a big wrench
for us, but it were no good struggling against
what was to be. So we shook hands and parted on
it quiet, and what became of Tom I have never
heard from that day to this, but like enough he
is dead years ago.

"Well, it would be too long a story to tell you
all that happened in the nine months I stopped
in that village. The chief was very proud of me,
and used to show me off to his visitors. I had

not such a very bad time of it. I used to make myself as useful as I could. I had been a handy sort of chap, and fond of carpentry, and I made a shift with what native tools I could get to turn out tables and chairs, and cupboards, and such like. All this time I was wondering how I was ever to get back again. I used to share a hut with another slave who had been captured in war. They generally sell them to the Arab slave-dealers to take down to the coast, but this man was the son of a chief who had gone to war with the fellow who owned me, and had been killed; and he kept this chap as his slave as a sort of brag, I think.

"We got on very well together, and of course by the time we had been there six months I got to talk their lingo, and we agreed at last that we would try to make a bolt of it together. So one night—when it happened that there was a great feast in the village—we slipped away as soon as it got dark, and made south, our object being to strike one of the Portuguese stations. We armed ourselves with bows and arrows, and spears; and as many yams as we could carry. It would make a book, lads, if I was to tell you all we went through before we got there. We travelled chiefly by nights; sometimes killing a deer, sometimes getting a few yams or heads of corn from the fields of the villages we passed. We had one or two skrimages, but fortunately never ran against any strong bodies of natives. By myself I should have died before I had been gone a fortnight, but Mwango was up to every dodge. He knew what roots were good to eat, and what fruit and berries were safe. He could steal up to a herd of deer without frightening them, and was a first-rate hand in making pitfalls for game.

"I didn't keep no account of time, but it was somewhere about six weeks after we had started when we came down on the banks of a biggish river. We followed it down until, two or three days later, we came on a village. There we stole a canoe, and paddling at night and lying up in the day, we came after about a week to a Portuguese post. There we were kindly received, and stopped for a month; and then I went down the river with some traders to the coast, while Mwango took service with the Portuguese. Six weeks later I was lucky enough to get a ship bound for the Cape, and there shifted into another for England. So that, young gentlemen, was the second time as I was off the books of Godstone & Son."

"Thank you very much, Joe. Some day you must give us some more yarns about it, and tell us something of your life in the village and your journey."

"I will think it over, Master Jim. It is a long time ago now, for I war not above six-and-twenty when it happened. But I will think it over, and see if I can call back something worth telling."

From that time onwards the boys had no reason to complain of dulness.

If the old man's memory ever played him false, his imagination never failed him. Story followed story in almost unbroken sequence, so that between old Joe's yarns and the ordinary duties of sea life the time passed swiftly and pleasantly. After rounding the Cape they had a spell of fine weather, until one morning when Jack came on deck he saw land away on the port beam.

"There is Ceylon," Jim Tucker said.

"I should like to land and have a day's ramble on shore there, Jim. There would be something to see there with all that rich vegetation. A very different thing from the sands of Egypt!"

"Yes, and all sorts of adventures, Jack. There are snakes and elephants and all sorts of things."

"I certainly should not care to meet snakes, Jim, and I don't know that I should like wild elephants. Still, I should like a ramble on shore. I suppose there is no chance of our getting nearer to the land."

"Not a bit, Jack. I heard Mr. Hoare tell Arthur that it was very seldom we passed within sight of the island at all. Sailors are not fond of land except when they are actually going to make a port. The further they keep away from it the better they are pleased."

"Such splendid weather as this I should have thought it would have made no difference," Jack said. "I should be glad if we were going to coast up the whole way. Why, we have had nothing but a gentle regular wind ever since that storm off the Cape."

"Yes, but it may not last all the way, Jack," Mr. Timmins, as he walked past and overheard the lad's words, said. "There is no place in the world where they have more furious cyclones than in the Bay of Bengal. Happily they don't come very often. Perhaps there is only one really very bad one in four or five years; but when there is one the destruction is awful. Islands are submerged, and sometimes hundreds of square miles of low country flooded, the villages washed away, and a frightful loss of life. I have been in one or two sharp blows up the bay, but never in a cyclone; though I have been in one in the China Seas. That was bad enough in all conscience."

The wind fell lighter as they made their way

up the coast. They kept well out from the land, and had not sighted it since leaving Ceylon. So light were the winds that it was some days before Mr. Timmins told them that they were now abreast of Madras.

"How much longer shall we be before we are at the mouth of the Hoogley, sir?"

"It depends upon the wind, lad. With a strong breeze aft we shall be there in three or four days. If we have calms we may be as many weeks."

Another week of light baffling winds, and then the breeze died away altogether and there was a dead calm. The sun poured down with great force, but the sky was less blue and clear than usual. At night it was stiflingly hot, and the next morning the sun again rose over a sea as smooth as a sheet of glass.

"I wonder what the captain and the two mates are talking about so seriously," Jack said as the three lads leant against the bulwarks in the shadow of the mainsail.

"I expect they are wondering whether the pitch won't melt off her bottom," Jim Tucker said with a laugh; "or what will happen if all the crew are baked alive. I am sure it is pretty well as hot as an oven."

"The sky looks rather a queer colour," Jack

said, looking up. "You can hardly call it blue at all."

"No, it is more like a dull gray than blue," Arthur Hill said. "Hallo! What is up, I wonder?"

The captain had disappeared in his cabin, and on coming out had said a few words to Mr. Timmins, who at once went to the edge of the quarter-deck and shouted "all hands to shorten sail." The vessel was under a cloud of canvas, for every sail that could draw had been set upon her to make the most of the light puffs of wind. Some of the young seamen looked as if they could hardly believe their ears at the order; but Jack heard one of the older sailors say to a mate as they ran up the ratlines, "What did I tell you half an hour since, Bob: that like enough we should have scarce a rag on her by sunset."

The lads sprang up the ratlines with the men, for they took their share of duty aloft. Arthur's place was in the mizzen, Jim's in the main, and Jack's in the fore-top. The stunsails were first got in, then the royals and topgallant-sails. The men were working well, but the captain's voice came up loud from the quarter-deck, "Work steady, lads, but work all you can! Every minute is of consequence!"

Jack looked round the horizon, but could see

nothing to account for this urgency. The sun was nearly overhead—a ball of glowing fire, and yet, Jack thought, less bright than usual, for he could look at it steadily, and its circle was clear and well defined. From that point right away down to the horizon the dull heavy-looking sky stretched away unbroken by a single cloud.

As soon as the topgallant-sails were furled the upper spars were sent down, then the courses were clewed up and two of her jibs taken off her. "Close reef the topsails!" was the next order, and when this was done, and the men after more than an hour's work descended to the decks drenched with perspiration, the ship was under the easiest possible canvas—nothing but the three closely-reefed topsails, the fore-staysail, and a small jib Mr. Hoare and the third mate had been aloft with the men, and as soon as all were on deck the work of coiling away ropes, ranging the light spars, and tidying up began.

CHAPTER XVIII

A CYCLONE.

"WHAT on earth is it all about?" Arthur Hill asked his comrades as the three boys gathered together after the work was done. "Why, there is not a breath of wind. Is it all done for practice, do you think?"

Jim shook his head. "I expect we are going to have one of those cyclones Mr. Timmins was speaking about the other day, though I don't see any signs of it, except the queer colour of the sky. I expect the glass must have been going down very fast. There is the captain popping into his cabin again. Well, he is not long about it," he added, as Captain Murchison hurried out again and spoke to Mr. Timmins, who immediately gave the order, "Furl mizzen and main topsails! Lower down the fore-staysail!"

"Well, there can't be more to do now," Jack said, when the order was carried out, "unless we set to work to set them all again."

"Look, Jack!" Arthur Hill said, grasping his arm and pointing away on the starboard beam.

A wall of black mist seemed to hang upon the horizon, rising momentarily higher and higher.

"The squall is coming, lads" the captain shouted. "When it strikes her hold on for your lives. Carpenter, put a man with an axe at each of the weather-shrouds. We may have to cut away before we have done with it."

All eyes were now turned towards the bank of cloud, which was rising with extraordinary rapidity. Small portions of the upper line seemed at times to be torn off and to rush ahead of the main body, and then to disappear, suddenly blown into fragments. A low moaning sound was heard, and a line of white could be made out at the foot of the cloud-bank. The water around the ship was still as smooth as glass, though there was a slight swell, which swayed her to and fro, and caused the shrouds and blocks to rattle.

Louder and louder grew the murmur. Again the captain's voice was heard: "Hold on for your lives, lads!" and then with a scream and roar, as of a thousand railway whistles, the gale struck the ship. So tremendous was the force, that although the closely-reefed fore-topsail was the only sail that the *Wild Wave* was showing aloft—for the jib blew from the bolt-ropes the instant the squall struck her—the vessel heeled over and over until her lee-rail was under water. Further and further she went, until the ends of the yards were under water, and the sea seemed to Jack, who was holding on by the weather bulwark, as if it were directly under his feet.

He thought that the ship was going to capsize, and had not her cargo been well stowed she must have done so. She was now almost on her beam ends, pressed down by the action of the wind upon her hull rather than her masts, and had it not been that the boys had each at the last moment twisted a rope round his body, they must have dropped into the water, for the deck afforded no hold whatever to their feet. Jack felt completely bewildered at the noise and fury of the wind. He had thought that after the gale they had passed through south of the Cape, he knew what bad weather was; but this was beyond anything of which he had the slightest conception.

Looking round he saw Mr. Timmins clinging to the bulwarks, and making his way along with the greatest difficulty until he reached the sailor stationed with the axe at the mizzen-shrouds, he saw the man rise from his crouching position, and, holding on to the bulwarks, strike three blows on the lanyards. Then there was a crash, and the mizzen-mast broke suddenly off four feet above the deck and fell into the sea.

Jack thought that the vessel lifted a little, for he could see one more streak of the deck planking. Mr. Timmins looked round towards the captain, who was clinging to the wheel. The latter waved his hand, and the mate again began to make his way forward. He passed the boys without a word, for the loudest shout would have been inaudible in the howling of the wind. He stopped at the main-shrouds again, the axe descended and the mainmast went over the side. The relief from the weight of the mast and the pressure of the wind upon it was immediate; the *Wild Wave* rose with a surge and her lee-rail appeared above the surface, then she rose no further.

Mr. Timmins looked back again at the captain, but the latter made no sign. He could see that the pressure of the wind upon the foremast was beginning to pay the vessel's head off before it; as it did so she slowly righted until, when fairly before the wind, she was upon a level keel. Then there was a dull explosion heard even above the gale, and the fore-topsail split into ribbons. But the ship was now before the gale, and was scudding, from the effect of the wind on the bare pole and hull alone, at great speed through the water. As soon as she had righted the lads threw off their lashings, but still clung tight to the rail, and struggled aft till they stood under shelter of the poop.

"This is something like!" Jim roared at the top of his voice into Jack's ear. Even then his words could scarcely be heard.

Jack nodded. At present, even had conversation been possible, he would have had no inclination for it, for he felt stunned and bewildered. It had all taken place in ten minutes. It was but that time since the ship had been lying motionless on a still ocean. Now she was rushing, with one mast only standing, before a furious gale, and had had the narrowest possible escape from destruction. As yet the sea had scarce begun to rise, but seemed flattened under the terrific pressure of the wind, which scooped hollows in it and drove the water before it in fine spray.

Jack had read in the papers about tornadoes in America, and how houses were sometimes bodily lifted with their contents and carried long distances, and how everything above the surface was swept away as if a scythe had passed over it. He had heard these accounts discussed by the fishermen, and the general opinion in Leigh was that there was mighty little truth in them. The Leigh men thought they knew what a gale was, and what it could do. They knew that chimney-pots and tiles could be carried some distance with the wind, that arms of trees could be twisted off, and that an empty boat could be carried a considerable distance; but that a house could be bodily whirled away, was going so far beyond anything that came within their experiences as to be wholly disbelieved.

But Jack knew now as he looked round that this and more was possible. He felt the whole vessel leap and quiver as the gust struck her, and this with only one bare pole standing, and he would have been scarce surprised now had the ship herself been lifted bodily from the water. As to walking along the deck, it would have been impossible. No man could have forced his way against the wind, and Jack felt that were he to attempt to move from the sheltered spot where he was standing he would be taken up and carried away as if he were but a figure of straw. Presently Mr. Hoare came down from the poop and dived into the cabin, making a sign to the lads to follow him. He stood there for a minute panting with his exertions.

"The captain has sent me down for a spell," he said. "He and the first and Jack Moore are all lashed to the wheel. Sometimes I thought that all four of us, wheel and all, would have been blown right away. Well, lads, this is a cyclone, and you may live a hundred years and never see such another. You had better stop in here, for you might get blown right away, and can be of no good on deck. There is nothing to do. The wind has got her and will take her where it likes; we can do nothing but keep her straight. There will be a tremendous sea get up before long. The water at the upper part of the bay is shallow, and we shall have a sea like yours at the mouth of the Thames, Jack,—only on a big scale.

"Our lives are in God's hands, boys; don't forget to ask for help where alone it can be obtained. Now I must be going up again. Steward, give me a glass of weak grog and a biscuit. Do you know, lads, my sides fairly ache. Once or twice I was pressed against the wheel with such force that I could scarcely breathe, and if I had been pinned there by an elephant butting me I could not have been more powerless. That is right, steward, get me my oil-skin and sou'-wester from the cabin. You had better get a kettle on over the spirit-stove, so that we can have a cup of hot cocoa when we like. Now then, I am ready for the fray again!" and buttoning himself closely up Mr. Hoare went on deck again.

Jack Moore was the next to come down. "Captain's orders, steward. I am to have a glass of grog. Well, young gentlemen, this is a gale and no mistake. I have been at sea over thirty years, and never seed nothing as was to be compared with it. If you get through this you need never be afraid of another; not if you live to be white-headed!"

After Jack Moore had gone up Mr. Timmins and the captain came down by turns. Each took a cup of cocoa. They said but few words to the boys, and were indeed almost too much exhausted by the struggle through which they had gone to be able to speak. The boys gathered again under the lee of the poop and watched the scene. It had changed considerably; the wind seemed as violent as ever, but the sea was no longer kept in subjection to it, and was now tossing itself in a wild and confused manner.

Another half hour and it had settled in some sort of regularity, and was sweeping before the wind in deep trough-like waves with steep sides, resembling those to which Jack had been accustomed in Sea Reach, on a gigantic scale. Soon again these were broken up, and were succeeded by a wild tumultuous sea like a boiling cauldron. The vessel was thrown violently from side to side, taking water over, now on one beam now on the other, and at times shaking from blows as if she had struck upon a rock. So sharp and sudden were her movements that the lads could not keep their feet, and again made their way into the cabin. Even here it was necessary to shout in order to be heard.

"What an extraordinary sea, Jim! I never saw anything like it before."

"That is what it's from," Jim replied, pointing to the tell-tale compass hanging from the beams overhead.

Jack glanced at it. "Why, we are running due south!"

"Aye; and I expect we have been two or three times round the compass already. That is what makes this frightful broken sea."

"Well, as long as we keep on running round and round," Jack said, "there is no fear of our running against the land anywhere."

Jim was further advanced in the study of navigation. "You forget," he said, "the centre of the cyclone is moving along all the time, and though we may go round and round the centre we are moving in the same direction as the cyclone is going, whatever that may be."

For hours the storm raged without the slightest

signs of abatement. The sea was now terrific; the waist of the ship was full of water. Green seas swept over the vessel's bows, carrying everything before them, and pouring aft burst open the cabin door and deluged the cabin. By turns the boys made their way to the door and looked out.

"Come out, you fellows!" Jim Tucker shouted after one of these trips of investigation. "The men are coming out from the fo'castle. There is something to be done."

The boys came out and crawled a few steps up the poop-ladder, holding on for life as they did so. They did not attempt to get on to the poop, for they felt they would be blown away if they exposed themselves there to the full force of the wind. Looking round, the scene was terrible. The surface of the sea was almost hidden by the clouds of spray blown from the heads of the waves; a sky that was inky black hung overhead. The sea, save for the white heads, was of similar hue, but ahead there seemed a gleam of light. Jim Tucker, holding on by the rail, raised himself two or three feet higher to have a better view. A moment was sufficient.

He sprang down again and shouted in his comrades' ears, "Breakers ahead!" It needed no further words. The light ahead was the gleam of a sea of white foam towards which the vessel was hurrying. Nothing could be done to check or change her course. Had the mizzen been standing an effort might have been made to show a little sail upon it, and bring her head up into the wind to anchor; but even could this have been done the cables would have snapped like pack-threads. There was nothing for it but destruction. Jack followed Jim's example—crawled to the top of the gangway, and holding on by the poop-rail raised himself to his feet and looked forward.

Right across their bows stretched a band of white breakers, and beyond through the mist he could make out the line of a low shore. The lads descended again into the waist, and with great difficulty made their way forward to where the men were huddled together round the entrance to the fo'castle. They too had kept a look-out, and knew of the danger into which they were running and the impossibility of avoiding it.

"Is there anything to be done?" Jim Tucker shouted.

A silent shake of the head was a sufficient answer. The vessel and all in her were doomed. The officers were now seen leaving the helm and coming forward. It was a proof in itself of the hopelessness of the prospect. The vessel was indeed steering herself straight before the gale, and as there were no regular following waves there was no fear of her broaching to. The boats, that had at the commencement of the storm been hanging from the davits, were all gone or useless. One or two had been smashed to pieces by heavy seas striking them; others had been torn from their fastenings and blown clean away.

The long-boat alone remained lashed amidships on the deck. Jack pointed to her, but an old sailor shook his head and pointed to the sea. No boat could hope to live in it a minute. Once in the breakers it would be swamped instantly. The officers made their way forward.

"It is all over, lads!" the captain shouted; "but some of us may reach the shore on pieces of the wreck as she breaks up. We will get the long-boat ready for launching: some of you may cling to her. Now, lads, let us shake hands all round, and meet our fate as British sailors should do— calmly and bravely. At any rate some of us may be saved yet."

The crew of the *Wild Wave* had been a happy one. Discipline had been good, although every indulgence had been allowed the men, and all were fond of her officers. There was a silent hand-clasp all round, and then some of the sailors followed the officers to the boat. As they did so they knew well that the order was given merely to keep them employed, for that the chance of anyone being washed ashore and reaching it alive through the tremendous surf was small indeed. As they cut away the boat's cover they looked round, and a low cry broke from several of them. The ship was close to the broken water.

Every man clung to something and awaited the shock. In a few seconds it came. As she descended a wave there was a tremendous shock, followed instantaneously by a crash as the foremast went over the bow. Another and another, accompanied each time with the sound of rending timbers.

"Cut away the lashings of the boat!" the captain shouted, drawing his knife and setting the example. As he did so he touched Jack and pointed into the bottom of the boat. The lad understood him. He was to put in the plugs, which at ordinary times were left out to allow any rain-water to escape as it fell. Jack in turn touched Arthur, and the two climbed into the boat to replace the plugs.

As they did so a fiercer gust than usual struck the vessel. The lashings of the long-boat had just been cut, and the gale seized it and raised it in the air as if it had been made of paper. Jack and Arthur uttered a cry, and involuntarily clung for life to the thwarts. Over and over they were whirled. Confused, giddy, scarce knowing what had happened, they clung on. It was a sort of nightmare, and how long it lasted they knew not. Presently there was a terrific crash, and they knew no more.

CHAPTER XIX.

CAST ASHORE.

WHEN Jack opened his eyes he lay for some time wondering where he was and what had become of him. There were stars in the sky overhead, but the light was stealing over it, and he felt that it was daybreak. There was a loud, dull, roaring sound in his ears—a sound he could not understand, for not even a breath of wind fanned his cheek. At last slowly the facts came to his mind. There had been a great storm, the vessel was among the breakers, he had got into the long-boat with Arthur to put in the plugs, they had been lifted up and blown away—and then suddenly Jack sat upright.

It was light enough for him to see that he was still in the boat, but its back was broken and its sides staved in. Around him was a mass of tangled foliage, and close beside him lay Arthur Hill, the blood slowly oozing from a terrible gash in his forehead. Jack leaned over and raised him, and loudly shouted his name in his ear. With a sigh Arthur opened his eyes.

"What is it, Jack?" he asked feebly.

"We are saved, old man. We have been blown right ashore in the boat, and we have both got shaken and hurt a bit; but, thank God, we are both alive."

"Where are we?" Arthur asked, looking round.

"As far as I can see," Jack replied, "we are in the middle of a grove of trees that have been blown down by the gale, and the leaves and branches have broken our fall, otherwise we must have been smashed up. We must have been lying here for the last ten hours. It was just about six o'clock when we struck, for I looked at the clock in the cabin the last time we were down there; and as the sun will be up before long, it must be getting on for five now. Now, let us try to get out of this."

With the greatest difficulty, for they were still weak and terribly shaken, the boys made their way through the tangle of trees and branches, into which they had so providentially fallen. Both uttered an exclamation of surprise as they reached the edge of the wood: the sea was nearly half a mile away! A tremendous surf was still breaking, and for a quarter of a mile out a band of white breakers extended along the shore. There were no signs of the *Wild Wave*.

Scarce speaking a word they made their way down to the shore, with the faint hope that some of their comrades might have been thrown on the strand alive. A few bits of broken timber alone showed that a wreck had taken place; the rest had probably been swept by the current up or down the coast. They walked for half a mile and then stopped. The sea here had made a clean breach over the land, and extended as far as the eye could reach. Retracing their steps they were again stopped by a similar obstacle. Then they went inland, passed round the grove of fallen trees, and looked landward.

As far as they could see stretched a broad sheet of water, broken only by the branches of fallen trees. It was evident that a vast tract of country had been submerged by the storm, and that what was now an island upon which they stood had only been saved from a similar fate by being a few feet higher than the surrounding country. Every tree upon it had been felled, and the very surface of the soil seemed to have been torn off by the fury of the gale.

Scarcely a word had been spoken from the time they first reached the shore. The fate of their shipmates had depressed them profoundly, and as yet they could scarcely feel grateful for their own escape. Jack was the first to rouse himself from this state of despondency.

"Well, Arthur," he said, "things don't look very bright, but we must hope for the best. At any rate let us thank God for having rescued us in such a marvellous manner. It seems almost a miracle."

Both the boys were bareheaded, their caps having been blown away at the commencement of the gale, and they now stood with bended heads for some minutes silently thanking God for their preservation.

"Now, Arthur," Jack said cheerfully, "let us go down to the water and see how fast it is sinking. It was running like a sluice into the sea at both ends of this island, and I do not suppose that it will be many hours before it is gone. As soon as it is we must set out and make our way across to the land beyond it. We are sure to find some villages there and to get some sort of food after we've been down to the water. I vote we go back to the wood and lie down in the shade there. The sun will soon be unpleasantly hot, and as there is no chance of our getting a drink the sooner we are out of it the better."

The day passed slowly; the boys talked but little, and when they did so their conversation turned entirely upon their lost shipmates, for that subject occupied their thoughts far more than their present situation. Before night the water had so far sunk that only some glistening pools appeared where a broad sheet of water had before spread. Arthur was suffering much from thirst and would have started at once, but Jack persuaded him to wait until the next morning.

"We may tumble into deep holes full of mud," he said, "and should get on very slowly. Let us have a good night's sleep and start with the first gleam of daylight. We shall be able to get along fast then."

They found, however, that it was not very fast work; for the country had been cultivated and the soil was now converted into a soft mud, in which they sank up to their knees. Here and there as they went on they saw piles of mud and sunburnt bricks, with timbers projecting, and knew that these marked the site where villages or houses had stood. Among the clumps of fallen trees they saw bits of colour, and knew that these were the bodies of some of the natives. Here and there, too, they saw the carcass of a bullock. At last they found the ground under their feet much firmer.

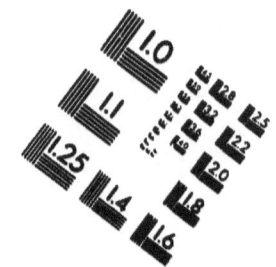

**IMAGE EVALUATION
TEST TARGET (MT-3)**

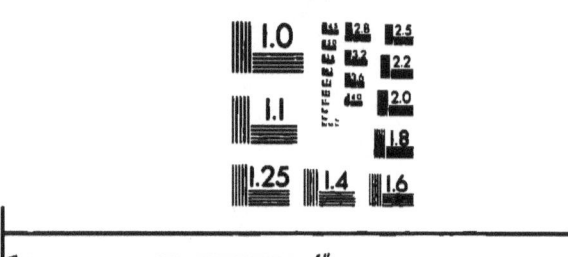

|←——————— 6" ———————→|

Photographic
Sciences
Corporation

23 WEST MAIN STREET
WEBSTER, N.Y. 14580
(716) 872-4503

"This has been a road," Jack said. "The flood as it went down has left three or four inches of mud on it, but it is fairly firm underneath. If we can manage to keep on this we shall get on well."

For six hours they plodded on, sometimes losing the path and floundering in the deep mud, at others regaining it and going along briskly. At the end of that time the mud was less deep, and in half an hour they were beyond the range of the inundation. Here and there a tree was still standing, and after an hour's walking they came to a village. All the houses were unroofed and many of them levelled to the ground, but the walls of a few were still erect; some natives were moving about, and a few were digging at the ruined houses, apparently searching for the remains of those buried there. They evinced no interest in the arrival of the two shipwrecked white boys, being too utterly cowed and broken to think of anything but their own misery.

"There is a well, Arthur; at least I expect it is that," Jack said, pointing to a post upon which was a long pole with a rope hanging from the end in the air.

They hurried to the spot, for both were suffering severely, and Arthur was scarcely able to speak. They found to their delight that Jack's surmise was a correct one, and hauling up the rope a bucket full of water came to the surface. Arthur was about to seize it, when Jack said, "You had better take this thing, Arthur; the natives might make a row if you drank from their bucket." Arthur seized the half gourd that Jack had picked up, dipped it into the bucket and handed it to Jack.

"Fire away, man; you are worse than I am," Jack replied.

The gourd had to be refilled two or three times before they were both satisfied, then they went back into the village. Jack pointed to his mouth, and made signs that they wanted something to eat. The natives shook their heads apathetically and proceeded with their work. At last they went up to an old woman sitting in a chair, and rocking herself backwards and forwards. She paid no attention when Jack addressed her, but upon his holding out a shilling to her her manner at once changed. She hobbled into the house and returned with a pile of flat cakes made from some native grain.

"We shall do now," Jack said, as, munching away at the bread, they tramped on. "We must get to some place sooner or later where there is somebody who can talk English. How much money have you got, Arthur?"

"I have got two pounds," Arthur said. "I took it out of my chest while the gale was going on. I thought if we were wrecked and did get to shore it might be useful."

"I wish I had done the same," Jack said. "I have luckily got a sovereign in my pocket, for I was going to pay Joe Scales for those six light canvas trousers he made me. Well, three pounds between us is not bad; and I have got four or five shillings loose, which will do, I hope, until we get to some place where we can change our gold."

They walked on till sunset, passing several other villages by the way. All of these had suffered more or less severely by the storm, but it was evident that as they got further inland the work of destruction had been less complete. At sunset they sat down in a grove of trees still standing, the first they had passed, and there spent the night.

"That looks a good-sized place," Jack said, as late on the following afternoon they came in sight of what was evidently a town of some size. "We shall probably find someone there who can speak English."

After crossing a bridge over a river they entered the town. They addressed several people, but these shook their heads and pointed forward.

"What do they mean, Jack?"

"I am sure I don't know, unless they mean there is somebody farther on who speaks English." Presently they came to a large house. Several people were passing in and out. Jack spoke to one of these, but he shook his head and pointed indoors. "This must be the right place, Arthur."

They went into a large room, where two or three natives were sitting writing. They looked up in surprise at the two travel-stained English lads.

"Can any of you speak English?" Jack asked. One of them at once left his desk and came forward.

"I can speak English. What do you want?"

"Thank goodness!" Jack exclaimed fervently. "We are two officers belonging to an English ship that was wrecked in the storm two days ago. We believe all the rest have been drowned. We have made our way on foot across the country, and you are the first person we have met who can speak English."

At the word "officer" the clerk had assumed a more respectful attitude. "The collector-sahib went away yesterday to see what could be done and what supplies are needed; he will be back this evening. If you will follow me I will take you to the mem-sahib, who will see after you."

Wondering whom they were going to see, the boys followed their conductor out at the back of the house into a large garden, in the centre of which stood a pretty bungalow. In the shaded verandah a lady was sitting reading. Motioning the boys to remain where they were the clerk went forward and addressed the lady, who at once rose. He beckoned to the boys, who advanced to her as she was coming forward to meet them.

"So you have been shipwrecked, I hear?" she said. "It was a terrible gale. We did not feel it so much here, but I hear the destruction on the coast has been awful, and they say thousands of lives have been lost. Pray, come in. My husband is away, but he will be back this evening."

The boys soon found themselves seated in easy-chairs in the verandah, while white-robed servants brought them refreshments. "Now," the lady said, "tell me all about yourselves. You belong to a ship that was wrecked; whereabout did she come ashore?"

"We have not the least idea," Jack said. "We had been hours running before the gale before we were cast ashore. We have been walking for two days, and have not found a soul who could speak English until now, so that we have not the least idea where we are."

"This is Cuttack," the lady said. "It is just outside the Madras Presidency. We are only separated from it by the river Mahanuddy. You must have been wrecked somewhere between the mouth of the river and Palmyras."

"How far are we away from Calcutta, ma'am?"

"About two hundred miles," she replied. "It is a low swampy unhealthy country all the way, but you will have no difficulty in taking a passage from here in a native craft. My husband will see about that for you. Where are your companions? You surely cannot be the only two saved from the wreck?"

"I am greatly afraid we are," Jack replied; "and we were saved almost by a miracle. I hardly expect you to believe me when I tell you." He then related the events of the storm, and the manner in which they had reached land.

"It is certainly extraordinary," the lady said; "but it does not seem to me by any means impossible, for I have heard that in these terrible cyclones houses have been taken up and carried long distances, and I can quite understand the same thing happening to a boat."

An hour later Mr. Darcy the collector returned, and after hearing the boys' story said he would at once cause inquiries to be made along the coast whether any white men had been thrown up alive.

"I fear that there is but little hope," he said, "for the surf on the coast in a cyclone like that we have had is tremendous, and even were anyone to float in on a spar he would probably be dashed to pieces when he approached the shore, and if he escaped that would be carried out again by the under tow. However, I will cause every inquiry to be made. The destruction has been terrible: numbers of villages have been swept away, and I hear that a great number of native craft are missing. Of course you will stop here for a few days with us to recover from your fatigue. I will rig you out until you can get fresh clothes made."

The lads stopped for a week under the hospitable roof of Mr. Darcy. No news came of any Europeans having been washed ashore alive, though several dead bodies were reported as having been cast up at various points. At the end of the week they were rigged up afresh, and Mr. Darcy procured passages for them in a dhow, bound for Calcutta. He laughed at the idea of the boys paying for their clothes or passage, and said he was only too pleased that he and his wife should have been of service to them.

They arrived at Calcutta without adventure, and at once reported themselves to the agent of the *Wild Wave* and told the story of her loss. Here again they experienced the warm-hearted hospitality which is so general in India, the agent taking them out to his house and installing them there until the next steamer was to sail for England. He had telegraphed upon the day of their arrival to Mr. Godstone, and received an answer requesting him to take passages home for them to England, where they duly arrived without any exciting incident.

Seven years have passed away, and Jack Robson is now second mate in one of Mr. Godstone's ships, and will be first officer on his next voyage. He has gone through many adventures since, but none approaching in interest and excitement to those which occurred on his two voyages in the *Wild Wave*. His mother still lives at Dulwich, and Lily is engaged to be married to Arthur Hill as soon as the latter attains the rank of captain. Jack is neither engaged nor married, but his mother has a strong idea that before very long he and Mildred Godstone will come to an understanding with each other.

Jack is always at the house when at home, and is treated by Mr. Godstone and his wife as one of the family. Indeed, Mrs. Godstone has as much as hinted to Jack's mother that she and her husband will offer no objection to the young sailor; but that, of course, they will wish their son-in-law to leave the sea and settle as one of the firm in London. Each time he is at home Jack makes a point of running down to Leigh and spending a few days there. "Sea-life is all very well, uncle," he says, "but for downright good sailing there is nothing in the world that to my mind beats a bawley."

THE END.

www.ingramcontent.com/pod-product-compliance
Lightning Source LLC
Chambersburg PA
CBHW032045230426
43672CB00009B/1474